AF304808

LEAN
SPARK

ADVANCE PRAISE FOR THE BOOK

'*LeanSpark* speaks to the India that is rising: resource-aware, ambitious and confident. Jaideep, Priyank and Mukesh weave research with powerful case studies to show how frugal innovation can drive national transformation. A must-read for entrepreneurs, innovators and investors shaping India's future' —**Sanjeev Bikhchandani, founder, Naukri.com**

'India's future will be shaped by aspirational innovators who can convert scarcity into strength. *LeanSpark* tells their stories with rare depth and clarity, and offers a powerful framework for policymakers, entrepreneurs and business leaders alike. It shows how frugal ingenuity, when married to science, technology and good governance, can transform not just India but the world' —**R.A. Mashelkar, author of *More from Less for More***

'*LeanSpark* pairs innovation with inevitable constraints and global thinking with a passion for real-world problem-solving. The spirit of the book reflects the kind of entrepreneurship we hope our youth will pursue, one that may begin small but strive for high quality and purposeful impact. Jaideep, Priyank and Mukesh turn India's legacy instinct for jugaad into a contemporary framework for designing solutions that can scale' —**Pramath Raj Sinha, chairman of the board of trustees, Ashoka University, and founding dean, Indian School of Business**

'India has both the opportunity and the responsibility to pioneer innovation that is affordable, scalable and humane. *LeanSpark* captures this mission with clarity and conviction, combining rich stories with a thoughtful framework for action. It is a timely guide for entrepreneurs, policymakers and business leaders who want India's rise to be measured not only in GDP, but in lives improved' —**Yusuf Hamied, non-executive chairman of Cipla Ltd**

LEAN SPARK

FRUGAL BY DESIGN
GLOBAL IN IMPACT

Jaideep Prabhu

Priyank Narayan

Mukesh Sud

PENGUIN
BUSINESS

An imprint of Penguin Random House

PENGUIN BUSINESS

Penguin Business is an imprint of the Penguin Random House group of companies whose addresses can be found at global.penguinrandomhouse.com

Published by Penguin Random House India Pvt. Ltd
4th Floor, Capital Tower 1, MG Road,
Gurugram 122 002, Haryana, India

First published in Penguin Business by Penguin Random House India 2026

ISBN 9780143480617

Typeset in Adobe Garamond Pro by Manipal Technologies Limited, Manipal
Printed at Thomson Press India Private Limited

www.penguin.co.in

Contents

Section II
LeanSpark Culture: Resource-Light, Impact-Heavy

Section III
LeanSpark Nation: Innovations Built to Scale

Behind the Spark
Authors' Note

It all started, as many good things do, with a question.

What happens when ingenuity meets constraint, not in a lab or a boardroom, but in the chaos of real life?

We were just three inquisitive minds pondering the same question, crossing paths at conferences and in classrooms and airports. Jaideep was chasing ideas across continents, from Bangalore to Cambridge, where he holds a chair in Indian business and enterprise. A decade earlier, he had co-authored *Jugaad Innovation*, a book that resonated deeply not just in India but around the world, opening new conversations about how creative problem-solving and resourcefulness could drive growth and transformation in emerging markets.

Priyank was at Ashoka University, building one of India's most vibrant entrepreneurship programmes. He taught through live projects and real-world messiness, constantly on the hunt for frameworks that students could not just understand but *use*. Which is how Jaideep ended up in his classroom; and one guest lecture soon turned into a recurring assignment. Conversations spilled over onto WhatsApp chats, email threads and a spark to do something more.

Meanwhile, Mukesh was at IIM Ahmedabad, thinking deeply about how innovation takes root in emerging economies. His research and teaching focused on entrepreneurship and innovation, and he often crossed paths with Priyank in academic circles, including as a visiting faculty at Ashoka University.

By chance, Mukesh bumped into Jaideep at Heathrow airport as they were boarding a plane to India. In the course of a conversation, they discovered they both knew Priyank well, a serendipitous connection that soon led to a shared project.

Before long, the three of us were co-teaching a course on frugal innovation at Ashoka that drew students from across the campus. Every semester brought new insights. Every assignment unearthed a story that made us sit up.

Mukesh and Priyank had worked together on a book titled *Leapfrog: Six Practices to Thrive*. Their collaboration with Jaideep deepened when all three met in Cambridge to plan this book in earnest.

We realized that our collective experience spanning research, teaching and industry had introduced us to a remarkable network of entrepreneurs who embodied the principles we wanted to explore.

We started with those we knew and admired. Chetan Maini, Jaideep's old schoolmate and the visionary behind India's first electric car. Rajesh Nair, who had taught in our classrooms. Manoj Kumar, who dropped by Jaideep's office in Cambridge en route to Delhi and left behind a trail of ideas. And others like Rahat Kulshreshtha and Vivek Raghavan, bold thinkers we had watched from up close as students, friends or colleagues.

Each person we met added a new thread to the tapestry, providing proof that lean, purpose-driven innovation is possible. We soon realized we weren't just writing about frugal ingenuity. We were writing *with* it, making the most of what we had: stories from our students, insights from our research, and conversations with a remarkable cast of entrepreneurs.

This book is as much a product of our personal journey and friendship as it is of academic research and classroom debate. It reflects the serendipity of chance meetings, the rigour of collaborative inquiry and the inspiration we have drawn from the entrepreneurs and change-makers we have been privileged to know. Our hope is that by sharing both frameworks and the stories, we can help readers understand not just the 'what' and 'how' of LeanSpark, but also the 'who' and 'why': the human spirit that animates every act of frugal ingenuity.

—Jaideep, Priyank and Mukesh

Introduction

India is at a pivotal moment in its history. It is now the world's fourth largest economy and is set to become the third largest in the coming decade. Powered by a young, ambitious population, India's growth rate over the last few decades has consistently exceeded 6 per cent per year, lifting hundreds of millions out of poverty and steadily improving lives. Yet, beneath these headline achievements, deep challenges persist. India remains low in global per capita income and human development rankings. Hundreds of millions continue to live and work outside the formal economy, lacking access to affordable banking, healthcare and education. Many Indians earn and spend daily, with minimal disposable income and little hope of attaining the lifestyles that much of the world takes for granted.

Resource scarcity compounds these challenges. India depends heavily on imports for energy and other key inputs. Land is scarce and expensive, and there is a shortage of skilled labour in many sectors. Even as investment flows into the country, the sheer scale of capital needed for full development is staggering. Infrastructure gaps remain, and the need to grow without depleting ecological resources is more urgent than ever. The central question facing India is this: How can it raise the standard of living for over half a billion people, given such profound resource limitations? How can it deliver growth without bankrupting its environment? In essence, how can India, long known for its jugaad innovation, scale these solutions to benefit its population?

This dilemma is not unique to India. In many ways, India is a microcosm of the world's developmental challenges. Globally, we face converging pressures of climate change, resource scarcity and inequality. By 2050, the world will need to meet surging demands for energy, water and food, all while navigating economic volatility, geopolitical instability and rapid technological change. India's struggle to deliver inclusive growth amid constraints mirrors these global challenges.

Introducing LeanSpark: The Book and the Approach

The answer we propose in this book lies in a new mindset and method we call **LeanSpark**.

LeanSpark is both the name of this book and the approach we believe is essential for the future. It is a contemporary framework for innovation that is rooted in frugality, adaptability and purposeful ingenuity. While it carries forward the spirit of jugaad—the Indian ethos of improvisational problem-solving—LeanSpark moves beyond makeshift fixes to solutions that are lean, scalable and sustainable.

LeanSpark is the intentional spark of innovation that emerges under constraints. It is about resourceful problem-solving that does not compromise on functionality, ethics or long-term impact. Instead, it thrives not despite limitations, but because of them. It is proactive rather than reactive, embedding sustainability and replicability at the heart of innovation. And this mindset is not unique to India or the developing world. In an age of climate crises, resource inequalities, digital disruption and geopolitical conflict, LeanSpark is a universal language of resilient ingenuity.

Indeed, the LeanSpark approach can be applied at many levels across companies, communities and countries. For companies, it provides a competitive edge in volatile markets, enabling faster, cheaper and more agile innovation anchored in real user needs. For communities, it is a tool of empowerment, turning scarcity into creativity and building solutions from the ground up. For nations, it offers a road map to leapfrog outdated infrastructure, deliver essential services at scale, and meet climate goals through ingenuity rather than excess. Governments can use LeanSpark to design policies and systems that are both frugal and future-ready, from space technology to digital governance. In a crisis too, LeanSpark provides a way to deliver rapid problem-solving when time, money and infrastructure are all in short supply.

Defining LeanSpark: The Four Key Attributes

At its core, the approach is defined by four key attributes.

Lean Execution: LeanSpark solutions are grounded in structured experimentation, iterative testing and continuous learning. This minimizes waste and maximizes learning from real-world feedback. In resource-scarce environments, investing heavily in untested ideas is risky and often unaffordable. LeanSpark draws on the principles of the lean start-up, emphasizing rapid prototyping, hypothesis testing and validated learning with customers to ensure that innovation is not only frugal but also aligned with user needs and market realities.

Purposeful Simplicity: LeanSpark solutions prioritize essential features and eliminate unnecessary complexity, without compromising value or scalability. Simplicity reduces costs, accelerates adoption and enhances scalability, all of which are especially important in markets where affordability is key. This is not about cutting corners but about focusing on what truly matters to users and removing anything that does not add value.

Adaptive Scalability: Solutions are designed to evolve and scale across diverse environments by flexibly adapting to new constraints or needs. The true impact of innovation lies not just in solving a problem once, but in enabling replication, localization and continued relevance over time. LeanSpark encourages organizations to build for flexibility and to leverage existing capabilities in new ways so that solutions can travel and multiply their impact.

Systemic Sustainability: LeanSpark ideas are powerful because they address root causes, minimize waste and create enduring value. Many quick-fix solutions fail because they ignore long-term consequences or systemic interdependencies. In contrast, LeanSpark embeds sustainability at the design stage, ensuring that solutions are environmentally sound, socially inclusive and economically viable. The focus shifts from temporary relief to transformative change that can be sustained and maintained over time.

Attribute	What it means	How it works	Key benefit
Lean execution	Disciplined experimentation with rapid cycles	Build–measure–learn loops	Faster learning, lower waste
Purposeful simplicity	Strip to essentials; complexity only when needed	Radical focus on core value	Lower cost, easier adoption
Adaptive scalability	Design to grow and evolve across contexts	Modular, interoperable architecture	Replicable without reinventing
Systemic sustainability	Minimize ecological and social externalities	Closed-loop thinking, waste reduction	Long-term viability, lasting impact

LeanSpark vs Jugaad: A Strategic Shift

This approach marks a strategic shift from jugaad. Where jugaad is improvisational, LeanSpark is intentional and strategic. Where jugaad delivers temporary fixes, LeanSpark aims for long-term, robust solutions that are scalable. Jugaad often circumvents systems and is hyperlocal, while LeanSpark works within ethical and regulatory boundaries and is designed for scaling and adaptation. Jugaad often ignores externalities; LeanSpark seeks to minimize environmental and social costs. Indeed, India is now at an inflection point, moving from a culture of jugaad to an era of high-tech, frugal ingenuity.

Aspect	Jugaad	LeanSpark
Mindset	Improvisational	Intentional and strategic
Durability	Temporary fixes	Long-term and robust
Ethics	Often circumvents systems	Works within ethical and regulatory bounds
Replicability	Often hyperlocal	Designed for scaling and adaptation
Sustainability	May ignore externalities	Minimizes environmental and social cost

Entrepreneurs: Engines of Frugal Ingenuity

Entrepreneurs are at the heart of LeanSpark. They are the ones who see constraints not as barriers but as opportunities, and build enterprises that are frugal, scalable and sustainable. In this book, we highlight the stories of several pioneering Indian entrepreneurs who exemplify this spirit.

Chetan Maini launched India's first electric car, Reva, and has since driven innovation in battery-swapping for electric vehicles (EVs), making sustainable mobility accessible and affordable. Rahat Kulshreshtha, co-founder of Quidich Innovation Labs, has transformed sports broadcasting by combining drones, AI and augmented reality, making advanced technology accessible for Indian and global audiences. Vivek Raghavan, a key architect of Aadhaar and now a leader in generative AI for Indian languages, is democratizing access to digital identity and artificial intelligence for millions. Lalitesh

Katragadda, creator of Google Map Maker and founder of Indihood, has empowered communities to solve local challenges through scalable technology. Deepthi Bopaiah, CEO of GoSports Foundation, has built sustainable support systems for athletes, enabling Indian Paralympians and Olympians to compete on the world stage.

These entrepreneurs share a common approach: they identify real needs, focus on core solutions and build for scale and longevity. Their work is not about improvising for the moment but about creating enterprises and systems that endure and can be adapted elsewhere. Their stories, and those of many others featured in this book, show how LeanSpark is already transforming sectors as diverse as technology, sports, retail, education and finance.

India's LeanSpark Moments

The Indian Space Research Organization (ISRO) has become a global leader in frugal innovation in rocketry, space travel and satellite technology. ISRO's achievements have spurred a thriving ecosystem of space-tech startups. Digital public infrastructure (DPI), such as India Stack and the Unified Payments Interface (UPI), has made the country a world leader in digital banking and mobile payments, spawning a vibrant fintech sector. Telecommunications is another area where India has excelled, offering some of the world's cheapest data rates and bringing the benefits of smartphones and the internet to nearly a billion people.

But for India to truly transform into a prosperous nation where the majority enjoy a high standard of living, it must do much more of this kind of innovation, leveraging technology and frugality together. This will require the creation of large numbers of frugal tech enterprises across sectors and across the country. That is the premise of this book.

The Next Decade of Frugal Ingenuity

Building on this premise, this book explores what has been achieved already and what lies ahead in the next decade of frugal ingenuity. We explore how the deep-rooted Indian mindset of jugaad is every Indian's superpower when allied with technology. LeanSpark in sectors like space, AI and quantum computing, education, energy, transportation and agriculture will improve lives at scale. We look at successful enterprises in these sectors and analyse the models that make them work. Drawing on these examples, the book develops a framework that can be used by new enterprises to create their own frugal innovations in high-tech areas. Our aim is not just to chronicle the transformation, but to enable and accelerate it, while warning of the pitfalls that will inevitably arise on this journey.

Implications Beyond India: Lessons for the World

While the book draws extensively from the Indian context, its lessons have global relevance. For other emerging economies, the key takeaway is how to innovate using limited resources; how to develop and deliver highly affordable solutions to large numbers of low-income consumers. For developed economies, long reliant on the capital-intensive Silicon Valley model, this book offers a counter-intuitive and sobering antidote.

It demonstrates that rather than throwing money at a problem, the smart way forward is frugal. As Ernest Rutherford famously said, 'Because we do not have money, we have to think.' We argue that by starting with the assumption that you must be frugal, and by economizing on all sorts of resources, not just capital, start-ups and large firms alike can create truly sustainable solutions.

Sustainability, in this sense, is not only economic but also environmental and social. Even if Western economies face fewer constraints on capital, they must contend with limits on other finite resources such as energy, rare earth materials and time, just as emerging markets do. Accordingly, we also draw on examples from other countries, including developed economies, to round out our Indian examples.

The Promise of LeanSpark

LeanSpark, then, is more than a method; it is a mindset and a movement. It is the intentional, disciplined and scalable application of frugal ingenuity to solve the world's most pressing challenges. By embracing LeanSpark, India and the world can build solutions that endure, adapt and improve lives for generations to come.

Section I

LeanSpark Ventures

Bold Ideas on Bare-Bones Budgets

India's innovation story isn't only unfolding in glossy glass towers or billion-dollar labs. It's also happening in dorm rooms, delivery kitchens, backstreets and maybe even inside some big boardrooms.

This section is about that India. The one where 'serendipity' isn't just a word, it's a strategy.

Take Rahat Kulshreshtha. His journey into entrepreneurship began not with a business plan competition but on a flight to Dehradun. His mother was seated next to Dr Pramath Raj Sinha, a founder of Ashoka University. That chance encounter led Rahat to join the Young India Fellowship at Ashoka. Years later, another bit of luck came his way: on an elevator ride in a Dubai hotel, he bumped into Mukesh, and they continued their conversation over breakfast. That's where the spark for his story in this book came from. And our very first interview as a team was with Rahat on a chilly but bright Cambridge morning at the Judge Business School. The book had officially taken off.

Chetan Maini, India's EV pioneer, is Mukesh's friend and neighbour, and also, coincidentally, Jaideep's schoolmate from Bangalore. Mukesh and Chetan were on their way to a pickleball game when Mukesh casually pitched the idea of featuring him in the book. After the third set, Chetan agreed.

Abhinay Choudhari's story takes us into the textile trenches. He's solving the *kapda* part of *roti, kapda aur makaan*. An alumnus of IIM Ahmedabad, like many of the change-makers we've tracked, Abhinay is leveraging constraints to his advantage in his chosen area of business.

Then comes A.B. Gupta, or just AB as he prefers to be known. On a drive through the streets of Indiranagar in Bangalore, Mukesh noticed a cheerful foreigner outside the Pizza Bakery enthusiastically welcoming guests. That was AB's secret sauce: creating experiences, not just products. As it turned out, AB was a classmate of our research assistant, Nikhil. One conversation later, he was in.

Gayatri Srinivas's story is of corporate origin, but with soul. She and Priyank go back a long way, and their kids are kindergarten besties. During weekend playdates, over juice boxes and Legos, Gayatri would often talk about work at her company using the word 'jugaad'. That piqued our interest. Hearing how a global giant channels LeanSpark thinking was music to our ears.

And finally, Lalitesh Katragadda. The man who helped convince Larry Page and Sergey Brin to bet big on a little thing called Google Maps for India. Reaching Lalitesh wasn't easy. Our messages followed him across time zones and WhatsApp threads. But when we finally heard his story, it was worth every ping.

These are not stories of unicorns chasing valuations. These are stories of grounded builders who design simply, act frugally and scale smart. People who don't wait for the perfect conditions to arrive. They just start.

In these pages, LeanSpark isn't a theory. It's a live wire.

1.1

Cleared for Take-Off
From Dorm Rooms to Drones

Rahat Kulshreshtha always wanted to be a filmmaker. Chasing that dream, he left India for London in 2007 and enrolled in a bachelor's degree in radio and TV broadcasting at the University of Westminster. He then returned to India and spent a year making music videos.

'I soon grew sick of doing that. Looking for fresh ideas, I went to Ashoka University as a Young India Fellow. It was meant to be a sort of gap year. We did twenty-six courses in one year,' says Rahat.

One of the courses was the 'experiential learning module' (ELM), a nine-month-long practical project that Fellows would continue to work on after graduation. For his project, Rahat wanted to work with India's public broadcaster, Doordarshan. But his roommate Gaurav Mehta discouraged him from doing so.

They tried their hand at entrepreneurship instead, exploring the world of drones, and started by renting a DJI Phantom One drone to capture dynamic aerial shots. They had no idea what they were doing or where they were headed with it all. The first thing they tried was to get a photograph from above the Noida expressway. 'We had a nine-month ELM, risk-free,' says Rahat. 'If our idea didn't work, Gaurav could return to the auto business, and I would go back to film-making.'

What began in a cramped dorm room in 2013 eventually moved to a modest office in Katwaria Sarai, South Delhi. In the early days, Quidich Technologies was just about flying drones for documentary shoots and broadcast relays. There were no big breakthroughs, just long hours. But this was only the beginning of something larger.

This chapter explores how Rahat, and others like him, have charted their course through uncertainty, applying the LeanSpark mindset to build businesses with ingenuity and hustle.

The Rise of Quidich

The 2014 general elections were in full swing. Rahat and his team went to Aaj Tak News and demonstrated how they could use a new drone to get aerial shots of election rallies. 'We began with a three-day contract, travelling on an election bus, "Destination Delhi". We soon convinced the channel that our team was doing a great job, and the three-day contract turned into a forty-five-day one to cover the whole election'.

Together the team figured out how to live stream from a drone. This had never been done before. Until then, no one had any idea what an election rally or an election bus journey looked like from above the ground. 'Basically, Aaj Tak took a punt on us. They said: Can you do this, and we said: Yes, we can. There were three of us there. We came out of the meeting saying: How are we going to do this? We had just committed to something, and now we had to do whatever was in our power to make it happen.'

That spirit stayed with Rahat and Quidich ever since. Time and again, they would say yes and then figure it out later. With every challenge, they turned to the LeanSpark mindset of relentless execution to deliver on promises that once felt out of reach.

The first job covering elections gave Rahat and Gaurav a lot of publicity and validation. Then followed a period of five years of chipping away at a variety of things: mapping roads and railways, from Delhi to Meerut, tracking cell phone towers, and so on.

They knew they were pioneers, often ahead of their time. In sectors like mining, they attempted to replace traditional surveying—typically done manually with tapes—with sophisticated drone-mapping technology. But this proved to be a leap too far for an industry accustomed to conventional methods. As a result, they learned an important lesson: innovation isn't just about advanced technology; it's about timing and addressing the right problems at the right time. Being too early can be as challenging as being too late.

Providence in Cricket

Quidich's path to sports innovation emerged almost accidentally, from an exploratory email. Cricket provided the ideal entry point. Despite having no prior intention of entering the sports industry, Rahat and his team quickly recognized cricket's potential, both in scale and reach. With its massive audience, cricket offered not just visibility but also opportunities for innovation. This pivot proved transformative, turning their venture from a technology company into a sports broadcasting firm.

'Our first jugaad in this new space was helping viewers see a stadium from the outside, giving them the whole sense of the stadium in the context of the city. At around that time, we realized that drones were getting commoditized. So, we came up with augmented reality from drones.' This allowed Quidich to showcase toss flips flying out of the stadium or aerial firework displays, adding a new element of spectacle to sports broadcasting.

This shift to sports technology was the beginning of another five-year phase that saw the Quidich team push the boundaries of what could be done in live sports. They introduced buggy cameras and remote-controlled cars around stadiums, enhancing the viewing experience by offering perspectives that were previously not possible during live sports events. Despite a small team of twenty-one operators and a dedicated tech specialist, they kept pushing the envelope to see what they could do. Many innovations followed. They created the Quidich Tracker, an AI-powered system mounted on stadium floodlights that tracks players twenty-five times per second, a global first. And they followed it with Hyper View, which analyses ball trajectories in real time, transforming both strategy and the viewer experience.

The year 2024 was a major milestone for Quidich. The start-up partnered with the International Cricket Council (ICC) and Apple to build a cutting-edge app for the Vision Pro headset. The idea was to bring together every bit of match data, including forty-five data points per ball, video and Hawkeye into one smooth, real-time experience on the cloud. And for its big debut, they picked the perfect stage: the high-voltage India vs Pakistan T20 World Cup match in New York on 9 June 2024.

Footsie with LeanSpark

In talking about his Quidich journey, Rahat frequently uses the word 'jugaad'—an innovative and frugal approach to tackle problems—to describe what they have done. Curious about how he is using the word, we asked what it means to him.

'I'm referring to a specific mindset of problem-solving. If a problem is thrown at you, you throw back everything in your power to find a solution. It is all about a combination of problem-solving under pressure, with passion. Under normal circumstances, when this pressure is absent, the same R&D could take forever. The pressure of a deadline forces you to use methods that are not standard practice,' explains Rahat.

Rahat's way of working is rooted in solving real problems. He brings deep passion to everything he does, and he isn't afraid to fail. He believes that setbacks are part of the journey and that failures often open doors to breakthroughs.

In the early start-up phase, what helped most wasn't a strict set of processes, but the ability to bring together people who shared a certain mindset. 'Processes are great for repeating things that have worked before. But when you want to build something new, like using AI in a fresh way or telling a more powerful story, rigid processes can get in the way. That's when a flexible, creative mindset becomes useful.'

Rahat illustrates this point with an example of how his team worked through tough challenges. For the 2024 T20 World Cup, Quidich promised to deliver a new product called Quick Flip. The idea was simple: convert regular TV video shots in a wide format into a vertical format that looks better on phones. What seemed like a small task quickly turned into a massive puzzle which in turn consisted of over 150 smaller problems.

The team now had to figure out everything from what hardware to use, whether to process the video on-site or on the cloud, what kind of AI to rely on, and how to make it all work smoothly and quickly. Each decision opened up new questions.

The only way they could make it happen was by staying flexible and open to failure. The team didn't just follow a plan, they worked together and kept adjusting their plans until something clicked. That mix of grit and resourcefulness, the LeanSpark mindset, is what helped them find a simple solution to a problem that had initially seemed to be overwhelming.

Serendipity: Luck and the Long Game

Entrepreneurs often start with a clear plan but rarely stick to it. As David Padwa, founder of Agrigenetics, once said, 'You start with a plan and follow it systematically. But even though you start out in the alternative energy business, you are just as likely to end up in real-estate development. That shift isn't random luck; it's serendipity at work.'

Serendipity, as researcher Nicholas Dew explains, is not just about being in the right place at the right time. It's when a purposeful journey meets an unexpected moment. For it to truly matter, the entrepreneur needs to be already engaged in the process, carry some prior knowledge or experience and be open enough to see new meaning in a surprising event.

Rahat's journey with Quidich is a classic example of this. He didn't set out to build one of India's most exciting sports tech companies. He started with a basic drone service, working small gigs. What set him apart was his openness to the unexpected: whether this was figuring out live drone streaming for political rallies, building real-time tracking for cricket matches or reimagining viewer experiences with AI. These leaps didn't come from a fixed plan. They came from chance encounters and unpredictable client demands that others might have turned down or ignored.

But Rahat didn't just stumble onto these breakthroughs. He had enough knowledge to recognize the spark in these moments, and the mindset to act on them. What appeared like accidental discoveries became game changers, because he was ready to make something of them.

Rahat's story is full of unexpected twists, starting with the Young India Fellowship. It was his mother who nudged him to apply, after a chance meeting with Ashoka University's founder, Pramath Raj Sinha, on a flight to Dehradun. Rahat wasn't keen on going back to college, but something about that moment made him rethink his earlier resolve and he eventually said yes.

That openness to chance followed him into his work at Quidich. He made it a habit to write 'future press releases' for himself, imagining what he wanted to achieve five years down the line. In one of these, he dreamed of doing something big with Apple. So, on a trip to Las Vegas, he tried to make it happen. After reaching out to everyone he could think of, he landed a breakfast meeting with a senior Apple executive in San Jose who led the firm's sports projects.

The meeting was short, a mere five minutes to talk about Quidich. And in fact, they chatted more about food and sport than drones or cricket. Afterwards, the whole thing felt like a missed opportunity.

A week later, everything changed. The ICC contacted Apple, saying they wanted to create an application that used the Vision Pro headset. The same Apple executive, who didn't even know much about cricket, remembered Rahat and told the ICC, 'There's only one company I'd trust with this: Quidich.' And that is how a random breakfast conversation turned into a major partnership.

Serendipity also showed up inside the Quidich team. As the company began to grow, it needed more structure. The founders did not want to lose their creative spark. One day, Rahat and his co-founder Gaurav were casually discussing how to track the ball's movement after it was hit. A teammate from the hardware team, who wasn't even part of the conversation, happened to overhear what they were saying. At home that night he thought about the issue and came back the next day with a four-page solution. This eventually became the foundation for Quidich's ball-tracking software.

None of this was planned. The team was open, curious and willing to figure things out even when it wasn't their job and big ideas took flight. The mix of being ready, being present and trusting a bit of luck made Quidich's journey special.

Scaling the Spark

What happens when hustle and heart meet systems and scale: Does LeanSpark still work? When Quidich first took flight, it was all hustle and heart. The scrappy energy gave Quidich its spark. Over time, as the stakes got higher, the company had to grow up. Could this mindset still work with bigger clients and a room full of expectations?

Turns out it could, but not in the same way it had before. As Quidich scaled, the mindset behind their innovation also evolved. Now it wasn't just about clever, inexpensive hacks anymore; it was about adaptive scalability. The team began building tools like the Quidich Tracker and Hyper View with this flexibility in mind. These weren't one-time quick fixes, but solutions designed to travel across sports, borders and use cases. Everyone was thinking beyond the prototype by asking: How do we design something that can grow, bend, stretch and still deliver every time?

Alongside all this, Rahat knew that endless frugality had to be supported by processes. What had worked in a start-up garage wouldn't fly in a live World Cup broadcast. So, the team shifted gears. They started building for systemic solutions that didn't just work under pressure but held up over time. This meant fewer shortcuts, more precision and more thinking about long-term value.

Rahat explains all this with an example from filmmaking. Making a movie needs a lot of creativity, but creativity alone is not enough. You also need clear roles, a proper schedule and planning sheets. Without that structure, no film can be made. He believes innovation works the same way. You need both the freedom to try new things and the discipline to stay on track. When these two come together, great things can happen.

Quidich has followed this approach from the beginning. The firm has grown from just two people to over 120 without any external funding. At the beginning, they received ₹10 lakh from Ashoka University. That taught the team how to work smart with limited funds. They have always been careful with money, and this has made them strong. Now, with more funds and a bigger team, they are ready to aim higher, but they hold on to the creative mindset that helped them begin.

Many start-ups like Quidich have used the fundamentals of LeanSpark to get off the ground.

Building Bold: How ePlane Is Hacking Urban Air Mobility

In the bustling streets of Bangalore or Mumbai, traffic is not just an inconvenience, it's a crisis. Ambulances stuck in traffic jams, office-goers missing meetings and people wasting hours crawling through the city. This is everyday life in many parts of India. The idea of flying cars has always sounded like science fiction, something only seen in movies. And for most people that's what it remains.

At IIT Madras, however, a small team is quietly working to change all that. This team is not building castles in the air or spending billions in the process. The ePlane Company, started by Professor Satya Chakravarthy and Pranjal Mehta, is attempting something different. They are keeping it simple and affordable. Instead of dreaming big with massive budgets, they are using what already exists and adapting it to build a flying taxi—the Indian way, with clever problem-solving.

Most air taxi start-ups around the world are working on large, complicated flying machines that need special take-off and landing spots called vertiports. In India, finding free land is difficult, and setting up new infrastructure can take years because of the need for government approvals and paperwork.

The team at ePlane had a simple idea: Why not use the rooftops of existing buildings? This small question changed everything. Instead of waiting for the perfect conditions, they worked with what was available.

Their aircraft, called the e200, is small and light. It doesn't need a huge runway or landing space. To build it, the team reused parts of regular planes and added electric fans to keep everything efficient. The goal wasn't to build the world's fanciest aircraft; it was to build one that could work on Indian streets and skies. Since they were based at IIT Madras, they accessed the students, professors and facilities that were already there.

One of their moves was realizing that the same aircraft could be used to save lives. In 2025, ePlane signed a $1 billion deal to provide 788 air ambulances to the International Critical-Care Air Transfer Team (ICATT), an air ambulance provider in India. Since their aircraft can land on rooftops and parking lots, hospitals don't need to build anything new to maintain this fleet. Patients can be flown quickly between hospitals, even during heavy traffic.

This isn't just about saving money, but about purposeful simplicity and lean execution. ePlane has already raised $20 million and received India's first approval for an electric aircraft from the Directorate General of Civil Aviation (DGCA), the country's aviation regulator.

The dream? By 2026, hundreds of these little flying machines will be helping people move faster, whether to get to work or to hospital. And all of this built not with billion-dollar budgets, but with the LeanSpark mindset.

From Frugal to Frameworks

Every entrepreneurial journey begins as a spark of energy. Turning that spark into something that lasts and scales needs more than just creativity. It needs a mindset of systemic sustainability.

Whether it's building flying taxis on a tight budget or streaming world-class sports coverage with homemade tech, the story is the same. At some point, passion and hustle must make space for process and systems. That doesn't mean losing the magic, it means giving it a backbone.

This is what LeanSpark is about. It's not just about scrappy beginnings, but thoughtful evolution. It's about designing innovation to be flexible enough to travel, and strong enough to stay. Because in the end, real change doesn't come from one brilliant prototype. It comes from building something that works and keeps working even when you're not in the room.

1.2

Wheels of Ingenuity

Low Cost Doesn't Mean Low Tech

Growing up in Bangalore in the 1970s and 80s, Chetan Maini found many opportunities to develop his skills as a tinkerer. 'I built my first radio in the fourth grade. From electronics, I developed a passion for flying.'

When he was in the fifth grade, Maini got permission from his parents to travel to Hyderabad to learn more about aircrafts. By the following year he had begun making remote-controlled planes. 'As a kid, I must have spent about 80 per cent of my free time building various contraptions. From radios and planes, I graduated to remote-controlled cars. My room wasn't just a place to sleep and study, but a workspace with all kinds of things I had made.'

With his father's help, Maini converted a balcony into a makeshift workshop. Complete with an asbestos roof, the workshop had various tools, including a milling machine. 'My next big project was to make a go-kart that I could drive around the neighbourhood. For this, I needed an engine, so I went to the junkyard and bought an old scooter. I stripped it down and used the parts to build my cart. I then sold the leftover scooter parts and made a profit.'

Maini's journey reflects the spirit of innovation that begins with curiosity, thrives on constraints, and transforms everyday limitations into launch pads. This chapter offers a glimpse into how LeanSpark ingenuity, when nurtured early, can evolve into scalable solutions that shape start-ups and industries.

Motor City, USA

Maini's early experiences of creating functional devices from limited resources laid the foundation for his future endeavours. In the late 1980s, he attended the University of Michigan for undergraduate studies. Choosing Michigan for its proximity to the automotive hub of Detroit, Maini immersed himself in both his engineering coursework and the projects that would shape his future career.

'I studied mechanical engineering, but I spent much of my time on extracurricular projects. In my first year, I worked on a "super mileage" car project, aiming to create a vehicle that could travel 400 kilometres on just 1 litre of fuel.'

This hands-on approach deepened in his second year when he joined the university's solar car project. This inter-university competition challenged teams to build a solar-powered car from scratch, pushing the limits of sustainable transportation. Maini was involved in every stage of development.

'At that time, I was working with General Motors (GM) as an intern. I would be at GM from 7 a.m. till 4 p.m., drive two hours to the Michigan International Speedway for testing, and spend four to five hours on the track.'

The effort paid off. The University of Michigan team, with Maini playing a key role, secured first place in the US solar car race from Florida to Michigan, competing against thirty-five universities. This success led to an even greater challenge: the World Solar Championships in Australia, where the team raced 3200 kilometres across the outback from Darwin to Adelaide against industry giants like Mazda and Honda.

On the first day of the race, the Michigan team finished ahead of Honda, shocking the automotive world. This experience instilled in Maini a sense of self-belief that would shape his future career.

After earning his bachelor's from Michigan, Maini chose Stanford to dive deeper into electric mobility. 'Stanford was one of the few places in the world that had special classes on smart product design, integrating mechanics, electronics and software,' he recalls. This interdisciplinary perspective sharpened his vision of a 'mechatronics world' where such technologies would soon become mainstream. At Stanford, he also built a hybrid-electric car, applying classroom theory to real-world innovation. These experiences armed him with the tools and conviction to pioneer India's first electric vehicle: the Reva.

Revving up to the Reva

While at the University of Michigan, Maini joined forces with three like-minded friends who shared his passion for electric mobility. After their strong showing at the Australian World Solar Championships, this group met regularly to explore business ideas. Through friends in their network, in 1991 Maini was introduced to Dr Lon Bell, a seasoned entrepreneur who had earlier founded and sold Technar, an advanced sensors company. Dr Bell, keen to launch a new venture, brought the group onboard his California start-up, Amerigon, to work on building an electric car platform.

Working at Amerigon, Maini began to realize the potential of electric mobility in emerging markets like India and China. And so, after government policy shifts disrupted the US EV market in the 1990s, he turned his focus eastward. 'I realized that the market would be in India and China,' he recalls. With encouragement from his mentor at Amerigon, he began exploring affordable solutions—an approach that would lead to the Reva.

'To make the new product suit the Asian market, we started looking at highly affordable solutions and rethinking every aspect of the vehicle to make it cost-effective without compromising on quality or functionality.' One such decision involved using flat instead of curved glass: ₹100 cheaper per unit. 'The US team didn't understand this, but I knew that in India ₹100 would make a difference,' Maini says.

Reva's ingenuity extended to testing. 'We needed to test the car for 75,000 kilometres, so we rented an empty field, made a track, and put a pole in the centre so the car could do circles,' he recalls. It cost little and worked well.

In 1999, at twenty-nine, Maini returned to India and transitioned from being a technologist to an entrepreneur. A friend from Harvard helped him write his first business plan on Excel spreadsheets. Raising capital and navigating an unprepared regulatory environment followed. 'We had to spend days explaining to insurance companies why they should do business with us. We had to be cost-efficient but effective.'

After seven years of R&D, the Reva was launched in 2001. 'Reva stands for Revolutionary Electric Vehicle Alternative,' he says, 'but more importantly, it was named after my mother, Reva Maini.'

The launch of the Reva in 2001 was a watershed moment for electric mobility in India. However, the initiative faced significant challenges from the start. Just months before the launch, the Indian government unexpectedly doubled the excise taxes on EVs and withdrew a subsidy of ₹1.05 lakh per car. This policy shift threatened to derail the entire project.

Despite the hurdles, the Reva made its debut on Indian roads in 2001. The first model was a compact two-door hatchback that could seat four people and was designed specifically for urban commuting. With its quirky design and zero-emission technology, the car quickly became an iconic sight on the streets of Bangalore, where it was manufactured.

The launch of the Reva marked the beginning of a new era in Indian automotive history. While it may not have achieved immediate commercial success, the car paved the way for future developments in electric mobility and positioned India as a player in the global EV market.

'I was young and naïve,' Maini admits, reflecting on that period. This naivety may have been an asset, however, allowing him to pursue his vision without being overly daunted by the challenges ahead.

From Reva to *Mahindra* Reva

In 2002, just a year after its India launch, Reva set its sights on the UK market. The company worked with a group of entrepreneurs to introduce the car in London, but this required significant modifications to meet UK regulations. 'We made over 130 changes to address regulatory issues,' Maini says. 'And in less than a year we launched the Reva in London.'

Reva's global journey took a leap forward with this move. Branded as the G-Wiz, Maini sold the cars online and serviced them through a mobile model: an innovative, frugal approach that perfectly suited urban needs. By the late 2000s, London had over 1000 G-Wiz cars zipping through its streets.

To showcase its tech leadership, Reva then unveiled the NXG in 2005, a concept EV developed in just four months. The new model, featuring a 200-kilometre range and tablet PC interface, won the Monte Carlo Sustainable Mobility Award. This gave Reva global prominence.

With venture capital secured in 2006, Reva then launched the REVAi in 2007, featuring AC drive tech and reaching over ten countries. Finally, at the 2009 Frankfurt Motor Show, Reva revealed the NXR and the NXG, both sleek, lithium-ion-powered models with a 200-kilometre range and bold global ambitions. Plans for 30,000 units a year and a second plant in India underscored how a small Indian start-up had grown into a serious player in the global EV race.

Despite global buzz and innovation, Reva struggled to scale in the wake of the economic downturn. Sales volumes didn't match the ambition. 'That's when I approached Mahindra,' Maini recalls. 'I said to them: How can I license and electrify all your platforms for you?' The timing was right. As the only Indian company present at the Frankfurt Auto Show, Reva had begun to draw global attention.

Mahindra responded with an even better offer: a majority stake. 'At that point, companies were investing 1, 3 or 5 billion in electric mobility,' Maini says. 'I said, it's a big boys' game, India was still not ready for that sort of investment.' In May 2010, Mahindra acquired 55.2 per cent stake in Reva.

'This was a significant milestone,' Maini reflects. 'We had been looking for a strategic partner in Mahindra, and in them we found someone committed to the future of electric vehicles.' With the backing of an automotive giant, Reva now had the muscle to scale, and the next chapter in India's EV journey was about to begin.

From Entrepreneur to Intrapreneur

May 2010 marked a new chapter in Chetan Maini's journey. Mahindra & Mahindra had by now acquired a majority stake in Reva Electric Car Company. 'The company was renamed Mahindra Reva Electric Vehicle Company and I went from being an entrepreneur to being an intrapreneur,' says Maini. 'It was a completely different world.'

This transition from entrepreneur to intrapreneur involved a fundamental shift in perspectives, particularly in problem-solving and leveraging existing structures to drive change.

Now chief of technology and strategy, Maini focused on scaling Reva's electric innovations across Mahindra's platforms. 'We wanted to electrify a broader range of vehicles,' he recalls. 'The goal wasn't just better cars. We were thinking about how to create an entire ecosystem that would make electric mobility more accessible and attractive to consumers.'

In this new role, Maini was keen to prove that it was possible to have a fully green manufacturing process without compromising on efficiency or quality. He turned his attention to fast-charging solutions and battery-as-a-service models that were barriers to EV adoption.

'We started thinking about separating the battery from the vehicle. This approach could potentially reduce the upfront cost of EVs and address concerns about battery life and replacement costs.' The thinking was no longer just about product development. Instead, it was about reimagining the entire business model of automotive manufacturing and ownership.

By 2015, Maini felt that the company was ready for its next phase of growth. So, he stepped down from his executive role at Mahindra Reva and took on an advisory position. This allowed him to explore new opportunities in the EV industry.

Here Comes the SUN

After stepping down from his role at Mahindra Reva, Maini took a year off to explore new opportunities. During this time, he worked pro bono for the government on policy matters related to EVs. It was through this that he began to see the potential for a new approach to electric mobility, particularly in battery swapping.

'I was helping Anand Mahindra on a few global projects and trying to understand where the world was headed,' Maini recalls. 'Then I came up with the idea of SUN Mobility.'

Maini had identified a key friction point in EV adoption: charging time. 'I ran every model on fast to slow charging,' he says, 'and realized that battery swapping would be quicker and cheaper.' In cities like Delhi, where auto batteries lasted only eight months, the need for a smarter solution was urgent.

Maini partnered with Uday Khemka of the SUN Group, and together they studied global failures in battery swapping, travelling from Japan to Israel. 'It was a cool idea, but we needed to understand why it wasn't working,' he recalls. Armed with insights and two patents, they launched SUN Mobility. This was a classic LeanSpark move: learn from global missteps, reframe the problem and build a nimble, scalable system from India for the world.

Focusing on impact, they began with high-emission sectors. Their modular system introduced one swappable battery type for two- and three-wheelers. 'That's 80 per cent of India,' he notes. An open architecture system allowed any original equipment manufacturer (OEM) to plug in, making adoption frictionless.

With 140 real-time data points per second and cloud integration, SUN Mobility wasn't just building hardware, it was building a future-ready, adaptive energy ecosystem. 'With Ashok Leyland we launched our first solution of robotically swapping a 600 kg battery in one minute,' Maini says.

Investors like Bosch came on board, with a $78 million investment and $200 million more planned. 'We've done 1.7 million swaps in twenty cities, and we'll double that in six months,' says Maini.

With operations in the Philippines, Africa and South America, Maini believes that 'our solution is designed and made in India for global markets'.

The LeanSpark Mindset

'We're making decisions with the early constraint-driven mindset, but ratifying them using technology,' reflects Maini. 'The real shift is in recognizing that low cost doesn't have to mean low tech.'

For Maini, affordability is a design goal, not a compromise. The aim is to make solutions accessible to the customer, without making the product feel cheap or compromised. This clarity of purpose echoes the focus of LeanSpark on purposeful simplicity, stripping away excess while keeping the essentials strong. Maini remains grounded in the values that shaped his journey: not just making do, but reimagining what's possible, and building solutions that are both lean and meaningful.

Maini places great emphasis on hiring people who have the LeanSpark mindset. He believes this mindset can be cultivated, especially in the right environment. 'In the US, in the late 1990s, we were working on a shoestring budget building the Reva. Our entire team was American, but everyone had a frugal mindset. After three years of working together, we were speaking the same language.'

A similar story has played out in China with BYD, which started making small batteries in 1995 for laptops and mobile phones. At that time, lithium-ion batteries were expensive, so BYD found cheaper materials and eliminated costly production steps. This brought the price down from $40 to under $12.

This smart, cost-saving approach helped the firm grow quickly. By 2003, BYD had entered the electric vehicle market, using their battery know-how to build affordable and reliable cars for China and India. The idea was simple: give people what they really need, without extra features, but still make it work well.

Together, SUN Mobility and BYD have shown that with the right mindset, solutions that are built with purposeful simplicity and lean execution can revolutionize markets globally.

Ambitions and Constraints

While a resource constraint mindset sparks creativity, Chetan Maini is clear about its boundaries. 'If you're always constraint-driven, you risk becoming myopic. You can't always bootstrap. Too little capital won't get you there, while too much can spoil you. The right balance increases the chance of success.'

As ventures grow, the challenge shifts from innovation to structured scale. 'A jugaad mindset helps early on, but as you scale, the mindset must evolve. Efficiency remains key, but unnecessary constraints can hinder growth. Some people develop a fixed mindset, resisting necessary investment.'

This evolution was visible in Reva's journey, where the leap from start-up to a corporate mindset required new systems, without losing the original spark. 'The team that gets you from 0 to 1 is not the same that gets you from 1 to 10 or from 10 to 100,' Maini argues. 'Jugaad is not a strategy, it's a mindset. Today we have highly affordable solutions that are also highly technical. The difference is in thinking that low cost doesn't have to mean low tech.' The belief that ambition and constraint can coexist is what LeanSpark makes possible.

Reverse Innovation at Renault Kwid

The idea of developing frugal yet high-tech ideas is not just an emerging market phenomenon. Auto companies from the developed world are getting on board as well. In 2015, Renault, a French brand known for its stylish European cars, was struggling to make a mark in India. The country's car market was dominated by Maruti Suzuki and Hyundai, both of which excelled at the art of building affordable, fuel-efficient cars for cost-conscious Indian buyers. Renault needed something that blended affordability with aspiration.

Instead of following the traditional path of designing cars in France and then adapting them for India, Renault did something bold yet truly LeanSpark. It set up a design and engineering team in India, tasked with building a car from scratch, specifically for Indian consumers. The challenge? Make it stylish and feature-packed, yet highly affordable.

The result was the Renault Kwid: a compact hatchback with an SUV-inspired look, a touchscreen infotainment system (a luxury in budget cars at the time), and an affordable price of under ₹3 lakh ($3500). The entire car was built using frugal engineering principles, where every part was optimized for cost and efficiency. The car's lightweight structure improved fuel efficiency; locally sourced materials kept the costs down; and the stylish design made the vehicle stand out.

When Renault launched the vehicle, it was an instant hit. Sales soared, and it quickly became one of Renault's best-selling models in India, securing 25,000 bookings within two weeks and 50,000 in five weeks.

The real surprise came next. Kwid's success in India caught the attention of Renault's global leadership. They immediately saw an opportunity. If Indian consumers loved this affordable-yet-premium car, why wouldn't buyers in other cost-sensitive markets?

Soon, Renault began exporting the car to Latin America, Africa and even parts of Europe. The same frugal engineering principles that made it a success in India helped reduce production costs in those regions, making it an attractive option for young urban drivers and first-time car buyers.

The Renault Kwid's journey from an 'Indian budget car' to a global success is an example of reverse innovation, where products from emerging markets are later adapted for developed markets. It demonstrated that great engineering doesn't have to be expensive and that some of the best innovations can come from the most unexpected places.

What started as a bold experiment to crack the Indian market ended up transforming Renault's global strategy, proving that a lean and creative mindset of innovation can drive success beyond borders.

Lean but Not Lacking

Chetan Maini's journey from a curious schoolboy building radios and go-karts to leading India's electric mobility revolution is an example of what happens when resourcefulness meets purpose.

LeanSpark is not about cutting corners, it's about sharpening focus. As Maini puts it, 'Jugaad is not just about making do with less. It's about reimagining what's possible and finding innovative ways to create value.'

The impact of his work stretches far beyond electric vehicles. The future belongs not to those with the most resources, but to those who know how to use and leverage them.

1.3

Start Small, Scale Smart

A Playbook for Contemporary Ventures

This chapter brings together two distinct but deeply connected stories, those of Abhinay Choudhari and A.B. Gupta. While one built a retail revolution with BigBasket, the other scaled customer desire for flavour and efficiency through Pizza Bakery. Split into two sections, the chapter explores how new-age entrepreneurs across retail and food and beverage (F&G) have harnessed modern business models that are lean, tech-enabled and customer-obsessed to grow, scale and sustain their ventures in a fiercely competitive landscape.

Resetting Retail

In 1997, Abhinay Choudhari graduated from IIM Ahmedabad. Like many of his peers, he stepped into a corporate career, as India's tech sector was then booming.

In the early 2000s, however, he took the plunge and launched his first venture, Style Country. It was a bold idea for its time, an online store for branded clothes and shoes, long before e-commerce had entered Indian homes. The model was simple: partner with fashion brands, use Gati for logistics, don't hold any inventory and deliver straight from warehouse to customer. But the ecosystem hadn't caught up. Online payments were clunky, delivery networks were patchy, and most people still preferred shopping in stores. Style Country shut down soon after being launched.

The lessons Abhinay learnt from that experience about supply chains, customer behaviour and the power of tech would quietly simmer over the next few years. So much so that when he eventually co-founded BigBasket, those early failures would help shape one of India's most successful online grocery platforms. This is his story.

Kirana vs Tesco: An Unequal Battle

After his first venture failed, Abhinay returned to the corporate world, working as an IT consultant in Singapore, the US and the UK. While working with Tesco.com in London, he noticed how easy and reliable grocery shopping was in the UK. Customers could check exactly what was available in which store and were assured of quality.

This was very different from his experiences in India. Kirana stores were unpredictable. They could shut without notice, had limited variety and often didn't issue receipts. Even modern supermarkets in India struggled. Real estate was expensive, shelf stock was low and weekend shopping trips took hours. 'If you had a list of ten items, you might find only seven. In places like the UK, you'd usually find nine or all of them,' Abhinay says.

Having grown up doing grocery shopping for his family, he knew these challenges first-hand. Now he began to wonder: How could India do better?

To address this, he created Shop As You Like. This was a new model in the country, an online store that didn't hold any inventory. His team built a system that connected to Metro Cash & Carry, a German B2B wholesaler, and pulled data on the top 5000 products every morning. If there was enough stock and quality, those items were listed on the website. Customers would place orders online, and the team would then buy the items from Metro and deliver them.

The business had its problems though. Sometimes Metro's stock ran out because other customers bought the same items, and this meant Abhinay's team had to source from other places like HyperCity. Eventually, they had to start holding some inventory of their own.

Another big hurdle was India's love for touch-and-feel grocery shopping, especially for fruits and vegetables. Over two years, Shop As You Like built trust by offering quality and convenience, something people hadn't imagined possible for groceries.

How could one create world-class systems with limited resources that can change the way people shop in the country?

'Technology has to be the backbone of such a shopping experience,' says Abhinay. 'But it can also be the stumbling block in any such venture.' So, instead of investing in expensive enterprise software, the team built their systems using open-source tools like Django. This allowed them to move fast and test ideas quickly, in the true spirit of lean execution. But Abhinay also knew that once the start-up reached a certain scale, it would need proprietary tech that would serve as a moat that others couldn't easily copy.

Now came the challenge of logistics. In the UK, he had seen Tesco's delivery vans with separate cooling zones for different types of groceries. In India, nothing like that existed. So, the team built one from scratch. They took a Mahindra Bolero, installed a refrigerated container and partitioned it. One section stayed at -18°C for frozen goods, another was kept at +5°C for dairy, all powered by a simple fan and thermostat system. With this customized van, they could deliver ice cream, milk and lentils, each at its own correct temperature.

It was purposeful simplicity in action, solving a complex logistics challenge with minimal resources, without compromising on quality. This was LeanSpark, not as theory, but lived and built on Indian roads, under real constraints, with real customers.

Transitioning to Big Basket

From April 2010 to the end of 2011, the venture ran under the name Shop As You Like. By late 2011, as interest grew and more co-founders joined, it transformed into BigBasket. With a new name and a sharper focus, the team continued using the Metro backend for a while, until it was time to scale.

In February 2013, they launched their first warehouse. It was a turning point. Managing their own inventory meant better control over quality, lower costs and higher reliability.

The makeshift phase had done its job of proving the idea. Now came the hard part: scale. And scale demanded structure.

Soon BigBasket was fulfilling 15 million orders a month. Its refrigerated warehouses and temperature-controlled trucks served kitchens across India. In May 2021, the Tata Group acquired the company, turning it into a unicorn and giving Abhinay the chance to exit.

But even during BigBasket's rapid expansion Abhinay kept thinking about what had drawn him to entrepreneurship in the first place. For him, platforms like Uber and Airbnb reflected a LeanSpark mindset as they hadn't built new assets but had instead found ways to unlock the hidden value in what already existed.

Early days of LaundryMate

After stepping away from BigBasket, Abhinay turned his attention to another daily hassle faced by Indian households: laundry. While still at BigBasket, he had tested a pilot in Gurugram to learn the ropes by building a basic facility and tech stack. This experience helped him understand the gaps, especially in speed and reliability. With these insights, he launched LaundryMate in Bangalore, this time with a fully centralized facility, in-house logistics and an express three-hour service, setting a new benchmark in an industry where three-day turnarounds were the norm.

The laundry business in India had long been unorganized and unpredictable. Local dhobis would follow their own schedule, sometimes mixing up clothes or returning them damaged. Prices changed from one street to another, and there were no proper care standards, especially for delicate fabrics.

With LaundryMate, Abhinay wanted to change that. The idea was to bring structure to the chaos. Every garment that was collected would be photographed and tracked. Services were clearly defined, whether it was laundry or dry cleaning, with quality controls in place. Customers could even choose how their clothes were returned: folded, on hangers, or carefully packed with clips and cardboard for travel. It was laundry, made dependable.

Just like BigBasket drew inspiration from Tesco, LaundryMate looked overseas to reimagine the business in India. A company in South Korea called LaundryGo had cracked the code with a system for pickup and delivery. There, laundry was returned on hangers (not folded) and customers used a special contraption for this that latched onto their front door. It had wheels, a lockable code and a compartment for hangers inside. Customers left it out at 10 p.m. with their dirty laundry, and in the morning, it was wheeled away by the pickup crew. Clean clothes arrived the same way at night, neatly hung, locked and ready for use at the doorstep.

'LaundryMate is now building a version of this for India, designed for the way we live and what we expect,' says Abhinay. Since most Indians prefer folded clothes, their hamper will have dedicated sections for it. The circular model will also bring down delivery costs, which are higher in laundry because of the need for both pickup and drop-off, unlike single-direction deliveries in e-commerce.

The real magic? Night-time pickups and drop-offs. No traffic. No waiting. No face-to-face interaction. LaundryMate is even in discussion with housing complexes about installing these hampers to be like mailboxes, so laundry can be done without the customer ever having to open the door to receive delivery.

The Scaling Dilemma

The stories of BigBasket and LaundryMate show how LeanSpark thinking turns ideas into scalable systems. Both started with clever, low-cost workarounds. But they didn't stop there. They have layered structure, repeatability and smart execution on top.

This is about using the jugaad mindset as the spark and then building the engine to scale. These ventures prove that world-class service *can* emerge from constraint, when innovation meets intention.

This is not jugaad *or* scale. It's jugaad, *then* scale. That's LeanSpark.

A Pizza Crust with Hot Brewing Chai

A.B. Gupta's entrepreneurial journey didn't begin in a kitchen; it began with a flop. His first start-up, Chance, was a quirky little app that let Twitter users have short video chats with their favourite influencers. It sounded promising, but the idea fizzled out. AB packed his bags and moved to Bangalore.

Between singing gigs and helping out at his family's modest travel agency, a new idea began to simmer. In 2017, without any background in the food business, AB and his brother Nikhil decided to launch a restaurant. And then another. And another. Today, Pizza Bakery, Paris Panini and Smash Guys are beloved brands with twenty outlets.

Did LeanSpark thinking help build food and beverage (F&B) ventures too, besides the tech ones? AB's story shows how even in the crowded, chaotic world of F&B, you can break through if you're willing to challenge old patterns. In this section, we explore the story of young India's favourite haunts: Pizza Bakery, Paris Panini and Chai Point.

From a Flop to the Flame

After AB's first venture, Chance, folded, he realized that the app had been too complex and clunky. Disillusioned, and somewhat dreading the idea of joining his dad's travel agency, he remembers thinking, 'Will I end up just another entitled kid working in the family business?' But instead of giving up, AB took the hard lessons with him. He learned the value of simplicity. The importance of building for real users. And how disciplined execution matters more than a flashy idea. These lessons laid the foundation for everything that followed.

During the day, AB helped run the family's travel agency. By night, he chased his passion for music. He performed on TV reality shows, even making it to the top eight on one that aired on VH1 and Colours Infinity. 'I got eliminated on live television,' he shrugs, 'but it led to paid gigs at weddings, bars and nightclubs all over India.'

Still, he wasn't satisfied. 'I always knew I wanted to build something large-scale,' he says. 'Music gave me a rush, but business is in my blood.' That drive led him and his brother Nikhil to their next experiment: a pizza place. They had no F&B experience, just a love for good pizza from their student days in the UK, and a hunch that nobody in Bangalore was doing it quite right. So, armed just with Google, gut instinct and a willingness to figure things out as they went along, they bootstrapped Pizza Bakery.

And it worked. Today, their ventures include multiple brands, Pizza Bakery being one of them. What powered it all wasn't just hustle. It was structured risk-taking, fast learning and thoughtful scaling.

Pizza Bakery to the Smash Guys: From Idea to Scale

AB and his brother had spotted a clear gap: good pizza was hard to find. They had no background in food, but that didn't stop them. 'We had no idea what we were doing,' AB laughs. 'We just loved pizza.'

This time AB applied the hard lessons from his failed tech start-up. Instead of building something complicated, he started simple. 'Forget the fancy stuff. Just make pizza. Give it to ten people. See what they say.' That was their minimum viable product (MVP) and testing process. It worked, and people loved it. One outlet turned into two. But as they grew, AB realized that hustle alone wasn't enough. Scale needed systems.

'You can't juggle your way to fifteen restaurants,' AB says. As they opened their second outlet, they made a deliberate shift from quick experiments to thoughtful, lean execution. It was no longer just about hustle; it was about building a machine that could run well and run far. That transition from rapid testing to planned scale is what kept Pizza Bakery growing, along with their other brand, Paris Panini.

AB's next move wasn't about pizza or paninis; it was about proving something to himself. Despite the success of his earlier ventures, a bit of imposter syndrome crept in. 'This had been too easy,' he confessed. So he launched Smash Guys, which was part experiment, part personal test.

It was also a return to performance. AB had always loved the limelight: from school events to reality TV. This time, he built the brand in public, using Instagram and social media to share the journey, grow an audience and turn entrepreneurship into a performance.

He picked burgers because, like pizza and paninis, they're easy to standardize and don't need fancy chefs. As he explains, 'Since we're not chefs, we pick categories with less art, more process. This allows us to hire inexpensive labour and scale fast.' That thinking shaped everything about Smash Guys. Instead of chasing gourmet perfection, he focused on food that could be made well, quickly and consistently. Burgers suited that model perfectly.

His boldest move was the way he launched the product itself. AB is generally sceptical of the usual cautious approach of testing in silence, tweaking endlessly and then going public. Instead, he just put it out there. 'Burger drops', as he called them, were pop-up tasting events where people were invited to try early versions of the burgers and give instant feedback.

He didn't wait to rent his own space either. He borrowed kitchens from friends in the restaurant business. He used existing equipment. He worked with what was already available. This helped him move fast, learn faster and build a following along the way. 'The menu wasn't built in a lab. It was built on conversations with people, reactions and honest responses,' he says.

AB applied lean execution through rapid prototyping and real-time feedback, running burger drops instead of waiting for perfect menus. He relied on purposeful simplicity, choosing a product that could be standardized. His strategy allowed adaptive scalability, that is, testing in borrowed kitchens, refining on the go, and scaling only what worked.

Smash Guys wasn't just a business, it was AB's way of proving that with the right spark, even burgers can tell a bigger story.

AB's experience has similarities to other new-age F&B entrepreneurs in India. Many of them are building on the same mix of sharp observation, a calculated bet and lean execution.

India Runs on Chai: Brewing Success at Chai Point

Amuleek Singh Bijral's life turned a new chapter when he noticed that while India is a country of tea lovers, the organized market for tea was almost non-existent. Indians consumed tea at roadside chaiwalas or made it at home, but there were few branded, consistent and convenient options available.

Amuleek saw an opportunity to create a scalable, organized tea chain by combining quality, convenience and technology. In 2010 he founded Chai Point.

Unlike coffee, which had a growing café culture in India thanks to players like Café Coffee Day and Starbucks, tea was largely seen as a low-margin, informal product. To succeed, Chai Point had to scale efficiently with limited resources.

Chai Point's first step was simplifying the product and service model. It focused on consistent taste by creating a standardized tea preparation process across all outlets. The menu was limited to core offerings like chai and light snacks to increase operational efficiency. And the outlets were designed for quick service. The focus was on takeaway and delivery rather than dine-in to minimize real-estate costs.

For IT, Chai Point turned to affordable, off-the-shelf technology rather than expensive custom-built solutions. With it, they launched Chai-on-Call, India's first chai delivery platform through an app in 2014. This enabled customers to place orders directly from their phones for quick delivery. To maintain quality and consistency without increasing labour costs, Chai Point introduced the Chai Cube, an IoT (Internet of things)-enabled tea-dispensing machine. The Chai Cube automated the tea-making process, ensuring consistent taste and reducing training time for staff. They focused on repeat customers rather than just walk-ins, increasing customer lifetime value.

Further, instead of opening large, high-cost cafés, Chai Point focused on high-footfall areas like tech parks, office complexes and transit hubs. They opened smaller-format kiosks rather than large outlets, reducing rental and operating costs.

Chai Point built its brand identity around the emotional and cultural significance of tea in India. It used storytelling in advertising and social media, positioning itself as the modern, accessible version of the local chaiwala. The slogan 'We run on Chai, India Runs on Chai' became a powerful brand statement, reinforcing the brand's deep cultural roots.

Today, Chai Point runs over 150 outlets across eight cities and has more than 300 Chai Cubes brewing tea in corporate offices, creating steady, recurring revenue. While the company has raised over $50 million in funding, its real strength lies in its LeanSpark mindset: start with a clear market gap, build smart systems, use tech to simplify and scale sustainably.

As Amuleek puts it, 'Scaling efficiently requires a balancing process with flexibility—build smart, automate where possible, and focus on repeat customers.' That balance of structure and adaptability is exactly what powered Chai Point's rise and what makes it a standout example of a simple innovation done right.

Takeaway: Buns and Brews

AB's and Amuleek Singh's journeys capture the spirit of finding smart solutions, moving fast and staying lean. As AB puts it, it's about constantly asking: 'Is there a quicker, cheaper, faster way?' That mindset isn't about cutting corners; it's about cutting clutter.

At the heart of their approach lies purposeful simplicity, one of LeanSpark's core attributes. Whether it was AB choosing food categories that needed more process than artistry, or Amuleek building smaller, no-frills chai kiosks instead of large cafés, they focused only on what mattered. They trimmed the fat. They avoided complexity. And in doing so, they built systems that were easy to run, quick to scale and tough to break.

While AB's experience has largely been in food ventures, he believes this mindset applies across sectors, especially in consumer-facing tech, where user feedback is immediate and unforgiving. Reflecting on his first start-up, Chance, he says, 'It's even more relevant in tech or anything involving user interface, when real people use your product.' As he sums it up: 'Speed helps. You can outrun people.' For anyone starting up with limited resources, not just a philosophy, it's a competitive edge.

* * *

Both Abhinay and AB believed that innovation didn't have to start with massive capital; it could start with a sharp insight and a bias for action. Abhinay reimagined everyday services like grocery delivery and laundry with lean, tech-enabled models. AB brought agility to the F&B space, constantly asking: 'Is there a quicker, smarter way?' What united them was a mindset of moving fast, staying frugal and putting customers at the centre. Their journeys show that you don't need to wait for perfect conditions to build something meaningful. With hustle, clarity and a LeanSpark approach, new-age entrepreneurs can reshape even the most traditional industries.

1.4

Not Just Another
Big Company Story

The Elephant Can Dance

Can being lean, the spirit behind LeanSpark, really survive inside a global giant?

Gayatri and Lalitesh say yes. Not just in theory, but in practice. One sparked bold, bottom-up experiments inside a Fortune 500 company and the other built maps for the world from inside Google. In two very different industries, they showed that LeanSpark isn't limited to start-ups or social enterprises. This chapter (in two parts) is their narrative of thriving in the belly of the beast, provided you are willing to rethink scale, trust your people and design for simplicity. These two didn't wait for systems to catch up; instead, they built new systems from within. Their stories show us that even the biggest organizations can stay nimble.

Driving Innovation at a Global Giant

Gayatri Srinivas didn't set out to join one of the world's biggest companies. Or to stay there for over two decades. Her journey started far from any corporate boardroom.

Born in Bangalore, she attended a boarding school in the Nilgiris that shaped her. She says, 'You learn how to lead, how to listen, how to survive. It built a certain muscle.'

That same muscle would later help her navigate the high-stakes corridors of a Fortune 500 company. But could Gayatri ignite LeanSpark within a giant global corporation?

Engineering First

Back in Bangalore, Gayatri enrolled at an engineering college. While most of her peers were chasing the dot-com wave, Gayatri did something different. She chose mechanical engineering. Not a typical choice for a woman in 1999. 'It was an odd stream to pick,' she laughs. 'But I was clear: I didn't want to write code. I wanted to understand how things worked.'

Still, as she reached the end of her degree, another truth became clear: she didn't want a purely technical job either. What she wanted was to blend logic with storytelling. Machines with markets. That led her to Mumbai and to business school, where she earned an MBA in marketing.

That's also where she landed a job at a global giant. What started as a summer internship turned into a twenty-year journey. Innovating from *inside* a mammoth.

A Corporate Career in Sales

Gayatri's journey began on the ground, in the dusty lanes of western Tamil Nadu. 'I started in sales,' she says. 'Not from a plush corner office, but out in the market, face to face with retailers.' And it was there that she learned the ropes. But the real test came when she was moved to Haryana.

A woman. In sales. In rural north India. In the early 2000s.

The wholesaler was stunned. 'Why would HQ send *you?*' he asked. Not hostile, just completely unprepared. It wasn't personal. It was just that no woman had ever held that role before. Gayatri didn't flinch. She stayed and listened. Slowly, the shock turned into respect.

Then came Mumbai. Bigger city, bigger challenges. She stepped into trade marketing, helped launch the a new brand, and built a reputation for being someone who could get things done. Other roles included a stint in the USA. From dusty Indian streets to American highways, she'd come a long way.

What makes Gayatri's story powerful isn't just the titles she's held. It's a story of balancing structure with speed in getting things done in a sprawling legacy organization.

Who Says Elephants Can't Dance?

Big companies move slowly. Too many layers and approvals and too many people asking, 'Who signed off on this?' Gayatri has lived in that world. For her, working at a large corporate has often meant figuring out how to *move* inside a giant machine without getting stuck in its gears.

'Cost isn't our biggest problem,' she says. 'It's the layers of process and approvals. That's where things get stuck.' She calls it the elephant that needs to learn how to dance.

At the heart of it is the matrix structure, the typical way of organizing people across functions and geographies. When it works, it's brilliant. It sparks healthy debate. It brings different perspectives together to build better decisions. But when it doesn't, it slows everything down. Meetings for the sake of meetings. Approvals on top of approvals. Good ideas that get stuck in limbo.

So how does one get things moving?

The 70–20–10 Rule: 'Seventy per cent of your time,' she says, 'goes into the grind. Firefighting. Managing processes. Doing the stuff that pays your salary.' But that's not where the magic happens. 'The next 20 per cent: that's where you pause. Step back. Think bigger. What's the next leap? What's the next smart play?'

And the final 10 per cent? 'That's for the absolutely crazy stuff. The wild, out-there ideas. Most won't work. But some might just change everything.'

It's not just a time-management hack. It's a mindset. A way to make sure that even in the most structured, high-pressure environments, there's always space for innovation, creativity and just a little madness.

Bringing Start-Up Chaos into the Corporate: 'To me, a leader is someone who can make things happen—wherever they are,' she says. That means being adaptable. Reading the room. Changing gears when needed. One of Gayatri's boldest moves was bringing a semblance of start-up chaos into corporate culture.

While leading the company's India business, she launched an internal Shark Tank. No outside consultants. No big budgets. Just people with ideas and the guts to pitch them. 'I told everyone we're doing a Shark Tank,' she says. 'Bring your ideas. Convince the room.'

Innovation doesn't have to come from the top. Or wait for perfect conditions. It can be sparked by anyone if you create the right space. By mixing entrepreneurial energy with corporate muscle, Gayatri made room for wild thinking, start-up style.

Appreciating the Power of Less: When people think of a global giant, they imagine big budgets, big brands and endless resources. Gayatri flipped that idea on its head. 'One of our success drivers is what we call the scarcity mindset,' she explains. 'Whether it's time, money or people, you have to act like you don't have enough of it.'

'In my last role, no one really cared about this at first,' she admits. 'So, I created an award. Every quarter, we'd recognize the person who came up with the best productivity idea.' Within a year, everyone was thinking lean. People started seeing constraints not as roadblocks but as an invitation to innovate.

Choosing Chaos or Control

Gayatri doesn't shy away from the word 'jugaad'. 'I think jugaad got a bad name,' she says. 'But if done with integrity and purpose, it can be powerful.' For her, it's simple: jugaad that bends rules or compromises ethics is not okay. If it delivers smarter, faster, cheaper solutions without cutting corners, that's innovation. That's LeanSpark.

'Jugaad is not a one-size-fits-all concept; it's a spectrum,' says Gayatri. Sometimes, a quick fix can unlock a breakthrough. Other times, it just creates chaos. The trick? Knowing when to flex and when to follow the rulebook.

'In some instances, a little frugality might be just what we need,' she explains, 'to quickly solve a problem or take advantage of an opportunity. In others, excessive reliance on jugaad can create chaos, inefficiency and even lead to long-term failure.'

As a leader, you can't lean too hard in one direction.

'It's our responsibility to be sensible in how and when we apply jugaad,' Gayatri says. 'Sometimes, a process that is well-thought-out and carefully structured works better. Other times, we need to embrace spontaneity. It's about striking the right balance.'

'The challenge lies in "processifying" the application of jugaad,' she says. 'This might sound like a contradiction at first. How do we bring structure to something that is fundamentally unstructured and flexible?'

But it's exactly that paradox where smart leadership lives. Leaders who succeed here don't pick sides—they *toggle*. They understand that innovation and structure aren't enemies. They're dance partners. 'By recognizing where we are on the jugaad-to-process spectrum, we can make more informed decisions on how to approach challenges,' says Gayatri.

That's LeanSpark: not about choosing chaos *or* control but knowing when to unlock one or the other.

Making Giants Nimble

Gayatri's story is proof that LeanSpark doesn't only happen at start-ups; it can thrive even in the most structured global corporations. It's not about breaking rules for the sake of disruption. It's about knowing *which* rules to bend and *how far*. It's about creating space for small bets, quick feedback and lean thinking, without losing sight of long-term value. In Gayatri's world, innovation is a habit, a muscle that gets stronger as you balance hustle with heart.

How Google Maps Was Made

On a precarious cliffside trail in the Himalayas, Lalitesh Katragadda found himself at the edge, quite literally. The ground beneath him crumbled with each step. Suspended between the trail and a terrifying drop, Lalitesh faced something deeper than fear. 'I had no choice but to be fully present,' he recalls. 'Each step demanded absolute focus. It was the first time I truly met myself.'

That moment didn't just mark his trekking adventure. It ignited a mindset of clarity and conviction that would eventually lead him to transform how a billion Indians see the world around them.

Born in Tanuku, a small town in Andhra Pradesh, Lalitesh is the son of a physicist who worked at the Tata Institute of Fundamental Research (TIFR). Books were his playground. Strand Bookstore in Mumbai was his childhood pilgrimage. While other kids played cricket, he lost himself in the geometry of galaxies and the logic of languages.

Years later, as a product lead at Google, he would notice something strange: large swaths of the world, especially in India, were still unmapped, omitted from the digital cartography that Silicon Valley took for granted. That invisibility bothered him. Which in turn led him to build Google Maps for India.

This is the story of the man behind the blue dot you trust every day. The quiet force who helped put India on the map, one pixel at a time.

From Bombay to the Bay

Lalitesh's journey began in Mumbai (Bombay) where childhood curiosity gave way to obsession. He didn't just want to build machines. He wanted to build systems and ecosystems.

He chased the future. He first did a master's in aerospace at Iowa State University, then a design degree at Stanford, and finally a PhD in robotics at Carnegie Mellon. In 1998, armed with a stubborn idea and without any business experience, he co-founded a robotics start-up called Sphereo in San Francisco. 'There were no robotics jobs then,' he says. 'If you wanted to build, you had to create the space yourself.'

For five years, Lalitesh and his co-founder coded, soldered and scaled. They engineered a massive, event-driven robotic system. The tech was promising and everyone loved what they had created. But when the dot-com crash hit, love wasn't enough. Their money dried up and the investors vanished.

A mentor offered a lifeline. 'Google,' he said. 'They see the world as a sensor system. That's exactly what you're working on.' Sphereo was ultimately acquired by Google in a fire sale amid the dot-com crash. Failure had taught Lalitesh more than success ever could.

When he walked through the doors of Google's Mountain View headquarters in 2002, he could never have anticipated that his biggest challenge, and greatest opportunity, was about to unfold. It came in the form of a deceptively simple question: How do you map a country as vast and complex as India?

The Unmapped Subcontinent

When Lalitesh set about establishing Google's first engineering centre in India in 2004, he realized that a crucial piece of the world's information was missing: maps. In a country of over a billion people, with 3 million kilometres of roads, and hundreds of thousands of cities and villages, the existing data was sparse, fragmented and prohibitively expensive to acquire.

Everyone agreed it was an important problem to solve. 'At that time, drivers all over the country would stop every 200 metres and ask for directions. Business could not locate where they had to deliver goods. When someone was sick, ambulances could not find them in time.'

When Google reached out to Microsoft and Yahoo to ask if they could pay for this together, they said, yes, that's a great idea!

'Maps at scale was an obvious miss in the internet space in the early 2000s,' says Lalitesh. 'So, we did the economic analysis and concluded that traditional approaches were economically unviable. At the rate of $10–15 per kilometre, mapping India's roads would cost a staggering $45 million. Even if this cost was split between Google, Microsoft and Yahoo, it was still an unsustainable investment.'

Moreover, considering India's rapid development, the country would require remapping every three to five years. Emerging markets were not quasi static like countries in Europe or the US where infrastructure development had happened for 100 years and was now almost done. 'In India, we would have to spend around $45 million every five years or so!'

This was also a problem that extended beyond India's borders. Across the developing world, from Africa to Southeast Asia, the lack of comprehensive, up-to-date maps was hindering economic growth, impeding disaster response efforts and leaving entire communities literally off the grid.

For Lalitesh, it was a challenge that demanded a different mindset. Rather than rely on expensive professional mapping services, he envisioned a tool that would allow local communities to map their own neighbourhoods, harnessing the power of the crowd to fill in the blank spots in the world's knowledge.

Larry and Sergey's Blessing

Lalitesh's vision for mapping the world found unlikely champions in Google's founders, Larry Page and Sergey Brin. In 2003, Lalitesh and three colleagues had written a white paper titled 'Universal Accessible Information'. It outlined the need to design and build products inspired by and for the emerging world.

This caught the attention of Larry and Sergey, who stumbled upon it on the internet. They invited Lalitesh and his co-authors to a meeting and offered unconditional support for setting up Google's first engineering centre in India.

'Larry and Sergey gave us two mandates for India. The first was not just to build a core tech centre for Google, but to create an entire ecosystem around it for tech-driven start-ups,' explains Lalitesh.

This was 2003. India was already the back office of the world. Tech giants like Microsoft had research centres in the country, but these were not doing product development yet. Other than GE, no one had built a core tech centre in India. 'We set out to build an entire ecosystem, for Google and for the country,' Lalitesh says. 'The first fifty people we hired were better than those in Mountain View. And subsequently lots of India's startups were ex-Googlers.'

The second mandate for Lalitesh, as joint head at Google India, was both ambitious and wide open: identify problems that are deeply relevant to India, yet which have the potential to serve the world. 'We were tasked with building products for the next billion users,' he recalls. But where do you start with a billion?

When the Google India office was inaugurated, Larry and Sergey were invited by President Abdul Kalam for a meeting at Rashtrapati Bhavan. At the meeting, President Kalam turned to Lalitesh and his colleagues and asked: 'Which of you will write code? I want to be able to type on my keyboard in English and Tamil should come out.' He was talking about transliteration, and Larry and Sergey immediately replied, 'Of course he will do it,' pointing to Lalitesh.

Immediately after the meeting, Lalitesh turned to Larry and Sergey and said, 'Do you realize this is a problem that research hasn't yet cracked?' 'So what,' they replied, 'that's what Google is for!'

It was the green light he needed.

From then on, the team got to work on solving the transliteration problem. They built a machine-learning model and launched Google's transliteration tool. It had taken them little more than a year to do so.

An Epiphany on Vittal Mallya Road

With support from Google's founders, Lalitesh moved to Bangalore in April 2004. His goal was clear: build a top-notch engineering team and solve problems unique to India and other emerging markets. What he didn't realize then was that mapping India would go on to transform how maps were built across the world.

The idea for what would become Google Map Maker came to him as he gazed out of his office window one morning onto Vittal Mallya Road in Bangalore. Watching the bustle of the city unfold before him—the auto rickshaws weaving through traffic, the locals navigating the labyrinthine streets—an idea struck him.

'We need to get them to help us build this product,' he realized, referring to the everyday experts who knew their communities like the back of their hand.

It was an insight rooted in his upbringing, in a childhood spent tinkering with circuits and building things from scratch. 'My dad would say that education is the art of learning how to discover, not the art of teaching,' he recalls. 'If you have to teach, it's a sign of incompetence, not competence.

'In India, people were used to doing complex things all the time without any training,' Lalitesh recalls. 'We used to fix our own circuits. At home, we didn't have a sofa, so our dad sat us down and we designed and made one ourselves. When TVs first came on the scene, people would install their own antennas. All this wasn't done individually; people did it together. There were no experts; people just figured things out.'

This everyday ingenuity—born of necessity and community—led Lalitesh to a design principle he calls 'nativance'.

Building on Don Norman's idea of intuitive design, which focuses on aligning products with natural human behaviour, nativance takes the concept a step further. 'It's about creating solutions that feel familiar right away, not because users are trained, but because the design fits seamlessly into their cultural and environmental context.' In essence, nativance is what happens when a product feels like it *belongs*—when it speaks the user's language, understands their constraints and leverages their local knowledge. It's not just intuitive. It's instinctive.

The Birth of Map Maker

With a small budget and a handful of volunteers, Lalitesh and his team began building Google Map Maker from scratch. They designed simple tools that allowed everyday users to sketch roads, mark landmarks and share local knowledge of temples, tea stalls, potholes and back alleys with just a few clicks. Behind the scenes, smart algorithms stitched this data into a seamless, usable map, while quality checks ensured the information stayed reliable.

Map Maker was launched in 2008, first in India, then followed by over 180 countries worldwide. It was a testament to the power of innovation on a shoestring budget. By tapping into the local expertise of millions of users, Google had found a way to map the unmappable, at a fraction of the cost and time of traditional methods.

Its real breakthrough was in the approach: building lean, designing with simplicity and empowering people to contribute from wherever they were. Instead of relying on top-down expertise, the solution emerged from those closest to the problem. The result was a system that could adapt, scale and endure as it was shaped by the very communities it served.

The Karachi Conundrum

One of the earliest examples of Map Maker's potential came from an unlikely place: Karachi, Pakistan. Despite the political tensions between India and her neighbour, Lalitesh and his team made a deliberate decision to launch Map Maker in Pakistan early on.

'The first map we made was in Karachi,' Lalitesh recalls. 'We couldn't manage the task from India. We didn't have the mapping policies; we didn't know the ground realities. The local community had to figure it out.'

It was a bold move, one that required a leap of faith in the wisdom and goodwill of the Pakistani mapping community. It paid off. Within weeks of its launch, Map Maker had begun to transform Karachi from a blank spot on the digital map to an intricately detailed tapestry of roads, landmarks and local knowledge.

Leading the charge was dedicated Pakistani mapper Farz Ahmed, who would come to be known as the power mapper of

Karachi. With over 5000 edits to his name, he was a one-man mapping machine, single-handedly charting the contours of his city with a level of detail and accuracy that no outside surveyor could match.

The power mapper's contributions went beyond just adding data to the map. In a lengthy email to the Map Maker team, he detailed the unique system of highway dividers used in Pakistan which differed significantly from those in the US and India.

Lalitesh and his team took note, verifying these insights and incorporating them into the Map Maker platform. It was a powerful validation of the ethos, namely, that the best solutions often come from those closest to the problem.

'The key thing is you have to listen to them,' Lalitesh says. 'We verified what he said and changed policies based on a single user.'

Google Maps was launched in Pakistan three months before it was in India. And when it was launched in India, Google's legal counsel warned that, given Indian laws, Lalitesh could risk going to jail for a few days. 'It's not strictly a law,' the counsel said, 'but they might cart you off, and I'll have to bail you out if they do!'

The Wisdom of the Crowd

When Lalitesh launched Google Map Maker in 2008, the Hyderabad team was tiny with just a few engineers and volunteers mapping thirty Indian cities. As the platform grew to cover 187 countries, so did the team. Over eighty people, including regional experts and community moderators, worked behind the scenes to keep the maps accurate and reliable.

In the early days, map accuracy hovered around 80 per cent. Decent, but not good enough for navigation. 'Wikipedia is about 60 per cent accurate,' Lalitesh notes. 'But if a map is wrong, you could end up in a lake or a wall.'

With steady improvements, the team brought the accuracy up to 98 per cent. After a few months, most edits could go live automatically with no human review needed. What started as a small experiment had become a global engine of mapmaking. And the Hyderabad team were the unsung heroes powering it all.

Scaling the LeanSpark Mindset in a Global Giant

As Map Maker grew from a scrappy idea into a global platform, Lalitesh faced new challenges. Culturally, some inside Google doubted whether a bunch of everyday users could really produce high-quality data.

As Map Maker gained success, the pressure grew to professionalize it by replacing community moderators with staff, charging for access and tightening control. But Lalitesh believed that doing that would destroy what had made the project work all along: the power of local communities helping themselves.

So, he pushed back. Armed with data, conviction and ground-level proof, he fought to keep Map Maker open and community-driven. Despite resistance from the top executives in Mountain View, he stood by the belief that real innovation can come from the grassroots.

'We had an epic battle which lasted six years,' Lalitesh recalls of his struggle with Brian McClendon, then head of engineering for Google Maps. McClendon questioned why people would contribute to maps voluntarily and expressed concerns about data quality and potential abuse of the system.

'Why will people do this?' Brian asked. 'Most folks are not that altruistic. And even if they want to do it, they won't be able to. I have to train people with geospatial degrees for four years to do mapping and you're saying a semi-literate auto driver in Bangalore can do the job?'

Lalitesh's response was, 'No, Brian. Some people *are* altruistic by nature and will help you, provided you give them an easy and fun tool to use.' This came from Lalitesh's conviction in the power of LeanSpark.

For his insolence, Google HQ would cancel the project several times. And still, he didn't give up. 'They were following traditional management techniques. We did not listen, and because we didn't listen, I was fired.'

In fact, Lalitesh was fired and rehired *four times*. Each time, Larry Page and Sergey Brin stepped in to bring him back. 'Brian eventually came around,' Lalitesh says. 'He told me, "I just couldn't see your world view. It was different." The key was to show results.'

More than fight to build a product, Lalitesh had to fight to preserve a spirit rooted in purposeful simplicity, community trust and lean execution. He became a cultural bridge, championing these values inside a complex system wired for precision and control.

By doing so, he proved that innovation at Google didn't have to come from the top. It could rise from the ground up. Even today, Lalitesh believes that big companies can stay nimble if they structure themselves right. 'Teams should be no bigger than 150 people,' he says, 'with leaders who operate like mini-CEOs.' It's a model built for adaptive scalability, where small, empowered teams can experiment, learn and build at speed, just like a start-up.

Lessons for a Flatter World

Today, as Lalitesh looks back on his journey with Map Maker and ahead with his current ventures Indihood and Avanti Finance, he believes this kind of innovation is more relevant now than ever before.

'Building products that work for 8 billion people is harder than building products for the elite,' he says. 'India will lead this kind of global innovation.' That's the spirit behind India Stack.

For Lalitesh, the future rests on three constraints: sustainability, affordability and nativance. In a resource-limited world, we must rethink infrastructure to be usable by all.

'The cell phone is the first deep-tech device that can be used by 8 billion people,' he says. 'But we still lack the language and systems to build scalable, sustainable tech for everyone.'

Through Indihood, Lalitesh is building platforms that let communities create their own digital tools—cheaply and locally. With Avanti, he's applying frugal innovation to bring financial services to the unbanked. 'Our current way of building tech is broken. It's too costly, too complex,' he says. 'We need a model that taps into community intelligence.'

Ventures built with simplicity and scaled by communities.

* * *

Both Gayatri and Lalitesh believed in small teams, fast feedback and empowering those closest to the ground. Gayatri did it by creating room for everyday experiments inside a global giant. Lalitesh did it by trusting ordinary citizens to build extraordinary maps. In their own ways, they proved that real innovation doesn't need to be big, it needs to be bold, local and human. When you listen closely and start small, even the most complex systems can shift. That's the quiet power of LeanSpark.

Section II

LeanSpark Culture

Resource-Light, Impact-Heavy

In the world of social impact, ambition often runs ahead of resources. The problems are large, and the odds aren't always even. This section is about the change-makers who didn't wait for perfect conditions or generous funding. They started with what they had. They stripped away the non-essential. And they focused on what truly moves the needle.

Meet Sanjoy Roy, the man behind the Jaipur Literature Festival (JLF). When he was invited to speak at Ashoka University, the response from students was electric. The story he narrated of bootstrapping what is now 'the greatest literary show on earth' was a masterclass in LeanSpark thinking.

Sahiba Bali is a promising actor and brand strategist. Mukesh's friend's daughter nudged us towards her, and once we heard her story, we understood why. Hers is a tale of zigzags and reinvention: from theatre to Shark Tank host, all stitched together with intent and agility. Given Sahiba's involvement with the Indian Premier League (IPL), it took several months to schedule an interview with her. The wait was well worth it.

We met Surabhi Hodigere with one big question: Can you succeed in Indian politics without a godfather? Her answer came wrapped in a humble Kannada phrase: *'Swalpa adjust maadi.'* Adjust a little, push forward anyway. This Harvard Kennedy School graduate is also involved with start-ups and has an interest in government policy. Her life is proof that conviction can speak louder than connections.

Then there's Manoj Kumar, the brains behind Social Alpha. Jaideep had known him before, but when we sat down to write this book, we saw just how much Manoj had achieved. Speaking to him drove home why we need many more like him to carry India's tech story forward. From entrepreneur to ecosystem enabler, his story is a road map for those who want to build not just start-ups but *systems* that sustain them.

Rajesh Nair didn't just *talk* innovation. He made our liberal arts students experience it first-hand. In a three-hour workshop at Ashoka, he had students soldering circuits, designing pet toys and rethinking what 'jugaad' means. His mission is simple but profound: to upgrade the image of jugaad from 'cheap hack' to 'clever craft'.

And finally, Shaveta Sharma. Priyank's work with Ashish Dhawan, founder of Central Square Foundation (CSF) and Chairman Emeritus of Ashoka University, had long kept him close to conversations on education reform. So, it was only a matter of time before we reached out to Shaveta, who now leads CSF. An IIM Bangalore alumna, Shaveta left a high-flying corporate career to take on one of India's most complex and overlooked systems of public education. Her work at CSF is powerful. Through policy and persistence, she's helping rewrite India's learning future.

Each story in this section is of a different kind. These aren't polished case studies. They're lived experiments in courage and conviction.

This is LeanSpark in its rawest and most real form: a way of moving through the world.

2.1

JLF

The Festival That Made
Literature a Movement

It's a crisp February morning in Jaipur. The kind that makes you linger outdoors, chai in hand, soaking in the winter sun. Outside the gates of Hotel Clarks Amer, there's a quiet buzz turning into a hum. Music, laughter, the chatter of a thousand voices. Banners flutter. Cameras click. JLF is about to begin.

Sanjoy Roy stands near the entrance, watching the crowd pour in. Around him, Namita Gokhale and William Dalrymple exchange greetings with friends, authors, schoolchildren and scholars. It's the festival's twentieth year.

Two decades since a small, makeshift stage hosted a modest set of talks in 2006. Two decades since an idea that almost no one bet on grew into the 'greatest literary show on Earth'. Back then, it wasn't a glitzy set-up. Just a handful of writers, a patchy sound system and empty chairs. What followed was a masterclass in creative problem-solving and cultural entrepreneurship. The team behind JLF found ways to grow the festival without growing its budget. They leaned on community, improvisation and relentless energy to build something far bigger than any one of them had imagined.

This chapter traces that journey from the first uncertain steps to the global phenomenon that JLF has become. It's more than a festival. It's about taking an idea rooted in scarcity and turning it into abundance. And how you build a world-class festival without losing your soul.

The Genesis of JLF

Sanjoy Roy started out in television. In 1989, he co-founded Teamwork Arts (TWA) with Mohit Satyanand, producing everything from soap operas to puppet shows. 'By 1995 we had about fifteen weekly shows running forever,' he recalls. But the grind took its toll. 'At a Saturday meeting, two of our senior colleagues said, "You know, we're brain dead." That was the turning point.'

Six years later, Sanjoy shut down TV production and returned to the arts. TWA platform Friends of Music supported bands like Indian Ocean and Parikrama. They backed new work in dance and theatre, giving artists a shot at projects they otherwise couldn't do.

Then came a visit to the Edinburgh Fringe Festival in 1999. 'Edinburgh is made up of seven different festivals,' Sanjoy says. 'I was convinced that's where we needed to set up our first platform.' TWA created a cross-festival programme showcasing India. Soon they were invited to Singapore, Australia and New Zealand.

Back home, Sanjoy was drawn into the Jaipur Heritage International Festival (JHIF), thanks to John and Faith Singh of Anokhi, who had seen his work in Edinburgh. In 2006, a small literature segment was added, with Namita Gokhale and William Dalrymple as directors. But by 2007, the festival was running out of funds. The Singhs asked TWA to take over.

'We signed the agreement on 9 December,' Sanjoy says. 'The festival was scheduled for 19 January. We had no money. No plan. Nothing. Somehow, we pulled it off in three weeks. I came down to the durbar hall and saw 200 chairs. I said, "Who's coming? Remove 100." But people came, you know. People came.' And they have kept coming.

JLF became a place where anyone could listen to the world's greatest writers without VIP barriers. 'No reserved seating for the *baba log, safed log*,' Sanjoy says. At the heart of it all was his core belief: *not* 'make do', but 'make possible'. 'In India,' he says, 'you're always getting an edge off. You're always trying to find your way around.'

Sanjoy's journey from television to theatre to global literature was never part of the plan. But it was guided by instinct, purpose and the belief that great ideas can bloom, even on a shoestring. 'We didn't set out to do what we eventually did,' he says. 'We just created platforms for people to explore, enjoy and spread culture.'

Building JLF

JLF's rise from being a small segment of a heritage event to a global literary powerhouse is a story of lean, smart management. A big part of its success lies in the teamwork behind the scenes. Namita Gokhale focused on Indian languages and emerging writers. William Dalrymple brought in global literary stars. Together, they struck a powerful balance.

As Sanjoy puts it: 'William had an international list, Namita an Indian list, and we were eclectic with our programmes. People knew Jaipur, it was a place for retail. All this made the proposition sexy. We added a touch of glamour and that got everyone's attention.'

That blend of depth and dazzle helped JLF stand out. It became a festival where bestselling authors and first-time poets shared the same stage. Where language, geography and fame didn't matter. Nothing captures this better than the story of a rickshaw driver who became a literary star, proof of how the festival opened doors for voices from every walk of life.

Manoranjan Byapari is a Bangladeshi Dalit who arrived in an Indian camp as a kid pre-1971. He was abused in the camp and ran away and joined the Naxal movement. Eventually he was captured and thrown in jail for twenty years. 'In jail,' says Sanjoy, 'the superintendent took a shine to him and trained him to read and write. He learned to read the notices on the prison walls and used a stick in the dust to write.'

In jail, Byapari must have read about 200 books. When he left jail, he was rehabilitated as a rickshaw puller. One day a lady got into his rickshaw, and he asked her the meaning of a difficult Bengali word. Where did you come across this word, she said. In a Mahasweta Devi book, he replied. At the end of the journey, she said: Show me the book. He pulled it out and showed it to her. She looked at it and said: 'I'm Mahasweta Devi.'

'So,' says Sanjoy, 'Manoranjan wrote a book. We heard about it and invited him to JLF. Back then he was a cook in a government school for Dalits in Howrah. He couldn't stand the abuse there and came to Jaipur for a respite. Meanwhile, he got some good press. The next year he came back with the English rights sold. By now he was a librarian in the school. The English launch happened, and notices appeared in the *Washington Post* and the *New York Times*. This led to translations into more languages.'

The book was translated into ten languages. Next, Byapari was appointed head of all libraries in West Bengal. Finally, when his second book came out, Mamata Banerjee, the chief minister of West Bengal, gave him a ticket to represent the Trinamool Congress. In 2021, he won the elections, becoming an MLA from Balagarh.

Challenges with Building JLF

When faced with unexpected challenges, Roy learned to improvise and find creative solutions. 'One year,' he recalls, 'there was a cloudburst in the middle of the night, and all the tents collapsed. This happened around two in the morning, and by 3.30 a.m., the entire site was in chaos. There was no standing structure left. It was a disaster zone. But our attitude was simple: yes, it's a disaster, we don't have electricity, no facilities, but we still have to start on time. So, the next day, we did everything we could to get things back in order. We explained the situation to our audience, and it created an entirely different atmosphere at the festival, earning us a lot of goodwill from those who attended.'

On another occasion, Sanjoy wanted the renowned percussionist Vikku Vinayakram to inaugurate their festival in

Singapore. The plan was for Vinayakram to travel by seaplane from Reunion Island to South Africa, then fly to Hong Kong, and from there to Singapore: all connections within a forty-five-minute window. Naturally, nothing went as planned. The seaplane was cancelled, so Vinayakram took a boat instead. Without a transit visa, Roy's team had to work with South African officials and then send precise instructions to Hong Kong and Singapore. 'Vikku, for his part, said he wouldn't eat until he was on stage with us!' Sanjoy laughs. 'And of course, in the end, everything came together.'

Reflecting on these experiences, he muses, 'At some level, the question is: Do you believe that something is possible? And once you do, you must invest that belief with not just hope, but also process, effort and common sense. Without those, nothing meaningful can happen.'

The mindset of building systemic sustainability has shaped JLF at every step. It didn't expand by chasing growth for its own sake. What truly sets JLF apart is how it has scaled without selling out. From day one, it has held on to its core values—free access, cultural inclusivity, literary democracy. That's systemic sustainability: not just growing wide but growing right.

Using Tech to Scale JLF

As the Jaipur Literature Festival grew, the team had to find smart ways to stay inclusive and sustainable without ballooning costs. A big issue was freeriding on food. People would pick up a plate, then pass their badge onto someone else. 'We were feeding 8000 people a day at our expense,' recalls Sanjoy Roy.

'So, we introduced a zapping mechanism; once you'd served yourself, your card couldn't be reused. This cost us ₹7 lakh to set up but saved us ₹14 lakh that year.'

Technology soon became central to the festival's functioning. 'We number crunch everything,' says Sanjoy. 'But we don't share our data. We're also moving towards zero waste; carbon offsets, no printed brochures. Tech helps make things affordable in the long run. It's expensive at first but gets cheaper down the road. So, we co-develop solutions with our tech partners, and they grow with us.'

This long-term, co-creative mindset of building scalable systems that are enduring pays off in the end. Maintaining accessibility while staying financially viable is a constant balancing act, however. 'Raising general ticket prices would exclude most of our audience,' says Sanjoy. 'And so, TWA introduced premium experiences through the Friends of the Festival programme to fund the rest of the event.'

Despite growing costs, the festival remained a democratic space. 'You could be sitting shoulder to shoulder with a Nobel Laureate or a Vikram Seth,' says Sanjoy. Namita Gokhale ensured the same diversity reflected on stage. 'There was a perception,' she says, 'that nothing was happening in Indian languages. But India was having a literary moment. It just needed a space for English and Indian-language writers to talk to each other.' Sessions on Dalit and tribal literature became a key part of the programme, giving space to voices often overlooked. As Sanjoy puts it, 'We made literature sexy. Now over 300 festivals have taken inspiration from us.'

Not every impact story from JLF is about scale. Some are about the reach. Sanjoy recalls one such moment: 'Some years ago, a tall guy came up to me and said, "I come from a small village 40 kilometres from Gorakhpur. I follow everything you do. I come here by train. I sleep at the railway station waiting room, and I come every day. And I'm so fascinated."' Moved by what he experienced at the festival, this village teacher returned home and started a small library with books he had picked up at JLF. He would teach children by day and read to adults in the evening. A few years later, he came back, this time not alone, but with eight or ten others from his village. Inspired by his journey, they had launched six more community programmes of their own in the village. This quiet ripple is at the heart of JLF's mission: democratizing access to literature and inspiring people to build cultural spaces of their own, no matter how modest the means.

Addressing Global Challenges through Culture

The global expansion of JLF reflects both its success and TWA's knack for adapting across contexts. As Sanjoy puts it, the idea was always 'to take India to the world and bring the world to India'.

The international journey began as a way to de-risk the main event. 'Around 2011–12, we realized we needed to de-risk Jaipur. One way was to move to London,' says Sanjoy. A partnership with the Southbank Centre followed, opening doors abroad. Oprah's visit had already put JLF on the global radar. 'Because of Oprah, all of America followed. We realized there was an opportunity in the US.'

But the team also encountered cultural blind spots. 'Post-COVID, we met Wells Fargo executives in Washington. One senior manager pointed to her notes and asked, "What is Delhi?" It's a city, I said. She asked, "Where is it?"'

'That's the opportunity!' Sanjoy adds. 'We obsess over the West, but they're not always thinking about us. So how do we introduce India to the world?'

The international expansion of JLF wasn't just about taking the festival abroad. It was about finding scalable ways to make it work. The team built touring circuits for performers.

'If we took Indian Ocean to the Perth International Festival, we'd follow it up with Melbourne, Sydney and New Zealand,' explains Sanjoy. This approach helped the team manage costs, increase revenues and extend reach without added managerial burden. A classic lean execution strategy.

The South Africa Story: From Violence to Vibrance

JLF's expansion into South Africa is an example of how culture can be used to solve local problems. As Sanjoy recounts: 'The city of Johannesburg had an issue. When apartheid ended and South Africa opened up, everyone from the rest of Africa arrived at the bus stop at Newtown, their central business district. This led to unemployment, violence and businesses moving out.'

Stephen Sachs, then head of the city, approached Sanjoy after hearing about TWA's earlier work in New York. Sanjoy's response was simple but bold: 'You arrange lighting and policing, and I'll walk around with a mobile in my hand and won't get mugged.'

The team outlined a plan. They marked out a precinct, brought in partners rent-free and helped establish museums. The result?

'Today, Newtown is one of the most dynamic, fastest-growing spaces in Jo'burg,' Sanjoy says.

This project showed how cultural interventions, when designed with intent, can revitalize urban spaces, reduce violence and spark economic renewal. A real-world case of culture being not just entertaining but transforming.

The Australia Story: Addressing Incarceration through Art

In Western Australia, JLF's approach helped to address a pressing social issue: the high incarceration rate of Aboriginal people. '2.2 per cent of Australia is aboriginal,' explains Roy. 'But Aborigines make up 98 per cent of the prison population. How do we reduce this? In Kalgoorlie, which has the largest open-cast mine, from cradle to grave, everyone goes to prison at some point.'

The team turned to art as a powerful tool for change. 'We asked community leaders to share their stories,' Roy says. 'It could be about the sun, the moon—anything that connected to their traditions, using desert materials as installation art. Each tribe had one core story, expressed in different ways, about how they understand the land, find water or survive on cactus.'

This creative project not only helped reduce incarceration rates but also became a way to preserve and celebrate Aboriginal heritage.

JLF's global journey shows how cultural platforms can be thoughtfully adapted to local realities while staying true to their core values. With creative thinking and sensitivity to community needs, the festival has managed to inspire real change in places far beyond its origins.

As Sanjoy says, 'JLF isn't just about song and dance. It's about creating value, both visible and invisible. It's about making a difference that spans generations, helping young people heal from trauma. That's been one of our biggest learnings.'

Controversies and Challenges

Over the years, JLF has had its share of controversies, testing its resolve to uphold free expression while operating within India's complex political and social climate. From as early as its third edition, JLF began attracting criticism, often for featuring voices that challenged prevailing political sentiments.

Roy notes that such challenges soon became routine. 'Every year, there was some controversy.' But instead of retreating, the team leaned into their values. 'We've never backed off. We have processes in place, and we try to be as compliant as possible,' he explains. That careful balance between courage and compliance has allowed JLF to preserve its identity without getting shut down.

One incident was in 2012, when Salman Rushdie's planned appearance triggered protests and security threats. Though Rushdie ultimately didn't attend, the controversy drew global attention. In a twist of fate, it also led to one of JLF's most high-profile moments. As Roy recounts, Deepak Chopra emailed to ask if Oprah Winfrey could attend instead. She did—and all of America followed.

Rather than being derailed, JLF used the moment to grow. 'There's nothing like bad press,' Roy reflects. In fact, many of these flashpoints, contentious statements and political tensions only increased the festival's global profile.

JLF didn't just survive controversies, it absorbed the shocks and emerged stronger. By staying true to its mission of free speech and cultural exchange, the festival transformed challenges into global visibility and long-term credibility.

* * *

While JLF has redefined how stories are shared and celebrated, it's not the only cultural platform reshaping India's creative landscape. Across the country, another bold experiment in accessibility and artistic ambition has been quietly gaining momentum. The Kochi-Muziris Biennale (KMB), rooted in the coastal heritage of Kerala, is showing how contemporary art can move beyond gallery walls and speak directly to the public. If JLF made literature democratic, the biennale is doing the same for visual art. But how did it rise so quickly to become one of Asia's most influential art festivals?

'Flexing Assets' at Kochi Biennale

In the bustling city of Kochi, where the backwaters meet the Arabian Sea, a bold idea took root in 2012. It was a vision to transform the city into a living canvas, showcasing art from around the world while celebrating local culture and community. This vision became the KMB, an art exhibition unlike any other, and a testament to the power of LeanSpark in the world of art.

The story began with a handful of artists, curators and cultural enthusiasts led by Bose Krishnamachari and Riyas

Komu. They believed in the transformative potential of art and also in the need for a new approach to creating cultural experiences. One that didn't require vast sums of money or extravagant infrastructure. They wanted to challenge the idea that art exhibitions had to be confined to glossy, white-walled galleries or expensive venues. Instead, they saw the historic town of Kochi, rich with colonial architecture, bustling markets and scenic waterfronts, as the perfect backdrop. They wanted to create a space where local culture could meet global contemporary art in a meaningful, accessible way. Their frugal approach, prioritizing collaboration over capital, allowed them to transform Kochi into a living, breathing art hub without the need for costly new venues, showing the world that true creativity thrives when it is grounded in resourcefulness and community involvement.

By leveraging the city's existing public spaces, such as old warehouses, schools and even defunct spice factories, the biennale was able to keep costs low while creating a truly immersive experience for visitors. The beauty of this approach was that it didn't just reduce the financial burden; it also brought art directly into the heart of the community. These spaces, once unused or underutilized, were transformed into vibrant galleries where visitors could wander through installations, sculptures and performances that spoke to the past, present and future of art.

KMB was more than just a festival of international art: it was a living, breathing collaboration. Local artists and communities were integral to the event, with their voices and stories woven into the fabric of the biennale. This wasn't just art on display; it was art that engaged with its audience. It invited conversations, evoked emotions and reflected the diverse cultural layers of Kochi. In doing so, it ensured that the art was relevant and resonated with the people who lived there.

One of the core principles behind the biennale's success was the idea of 'flexing assets'. Instead of building new, expensive venues, the organizers chose to work with what was already available. This was not only a cost-effective decision, but also an environmentally conscious one as it reduced the need for additional resources and construction. The use of repurposed buildings created a sense of historical continuity, where modern art sat alongside centuries-old architecture, blending the old and the new in unexpected ways.

Another key element was the concept of 'making innovative friends'. The biennale didn't operate in isolation. It tapped into a network of local businesses, government bodies and international artists to bring the event to life. By forging partnerships with local eateries, hotels and transport services, the event boosted the local economy while fostering a sense of community involvement. International artists were eager to be part of the biennale, drawn by its unique approach and its focus on grassroots collaboration. The result was an event that felt both global and local, where diverse cultures met in unexpected and exciting ways.

From its humble beginnings, KMB has grown into one of the largest contemporary art festivals in Asia. It has become a model for sustainable and community-driven art initiatives, demonstrating that innovation doesn't always require grandiose plans or hefty budgets. Instead, by rethinking how to use available resources, fostering local collaborations and embracing community engagement, the biennale has created a platform where art is not just seen but experienced in a way that is accessible, meaningful and sustainable.

Today, the biennale attracts artists and art lovers from around the globe, all eager to witness how frugal innovation can transform a city into a canvas, while simultaneously making art more accessible to everyone. Through ingenuity and collaboration, it has proven that creativity can flourish even in the most unlikely of places, and that sometimes the most profound impact comes from the simplest ideas.

* * *

The spirit of LeanSpark can be seen in different streams of the cultural revolution in the country. Film makers too have *leaned into* the spirit of frugal to create, scale and promote their films.

From iPhone to the Oscars: The Elephant that Roared

As a child, Guneet Monga was drawn to films. The spark came when she saw her mother's friend working on an international production. That brief encounter was enough for her to know that she wanted to make movies.

A neighbour suggested she start by filming local children. But Guneet thought bigger. 'Give me fifty lakhs,' she countered, 'and I'll go to Mumbai and make a film.' She was just twenty-one.

In Mumbai, she began the hard way. She convinced cameramen and light boys to connect her to directors. Nothing clicked, so she tried something bolder. She set up a stall in the food court of a mall. She put up signs and told passersby that she had ₹50 lakh but needed more funding to find a story and produce a film on it.

That audacity paid off. She teamed up with a director to create *Say Salaam India*, a feel-good cricket film timed to coincide with the 2007 World Cup. Funding came in through ad rights and cross-branding. But fate intervened. India crashed out of the Cup in the first round. Theatres, fearing angry fans and riots, refused to screen her film.

For Guneet, failure wasn't an option. She remembered how her school once charged students fifty rupees to watch a movie. She pitched an idea to her old Principal: let kids pay ₹50 to watch her film. She then struck a deal with a local theatre called Sapna for the morning slot. 'I will pay you double if you give me the hall,' Guneet promised them. She then got students to pay, collected ₹50,000 and gave Sapna ₹10,000. 'The profit was mine,' says Guneet.

The children loved the film, cheering and dancing during the film, and spreading the word afterwards. Guneet then scaled the model, hiring interns to pitch to schools across the city. 'That's how I became a producer at twenty-two,' she recalls. 'This is hustle. Saying, I have to solve this. And finding every way possible to solve it.'

Over fifteen years, Guneet's persistence broke barriers. She was one of the first Indians inducted into the Academy of Motion Picture Arts and Sciences. The *Hollywood Reporter* named her among the top twelve women in global entertainment. In 2023, she brought home her second Oscar, for *The Elephant Whisperers*.

That film began when Kartiki Gonsalves, a wildlife photographer, was driving through Mudumalai sanctuary, in the southern state of Tamil Nadu. On the side of the road, Kartiki noticed a frail baby elephant being looked after by a mahout and his wife. When she stopped her car, the mahout beckoned to her. The calf had been separated from his mother and was being brought up by the elderly couple. Kartiki was struck by the tenderness with which the mahout and his wife cared for the calf who was named Raghu.

Over several months Kartiki returned to the forest to get to know the couple better. She developed a bond with Raghu and the other elephant that the couple were nurturing. It was then that she decided to make a documentary about them. Unlike regular film-making that follows a strict timeline, Kartiki allowed the elephants and nature to establish the rhythm and flow of the filming.

Initially using just the camera on her iPhone, Kartiki followed Raghu and filmed his daily routine. It was only later that a professional crew was brought in. 'We did not have any sets; there were no actors and all we went in with was a lot of patience. It was unpredictable; we had to be there and not be there. We had to capture things and yet not go in with a large presence,' says Kartiki.

When Kartiki showed Guneet the raw footage, Guneet immediately saw what it could become. Sikhya Entertainment, the company Guneet had founded, stepped in, Netflix picked it up and history was made. *The Elephant Whisperers* became the first Indian film to win an Oscar for Best Documentary Short.

The process of making *The Elephant Whisperers* began with lean execution. Start with what you have: an iPhone, natural light and trust built slowly in the forest. And this was followed by purposeful simplicity with no elaborate sets or complex machinery; just the essentials, stripped to their core. Kartiki and Guneet turned scarcity into strength, and a local story into global history.

When Gatherings Become Movements

From the pink sandstone courtyards of Jaipur to the salt-laced air of Fort Kochi, India is rewriting the global playbook on culture. JLF and KMB are not just festivals, they are blueprints for how ingenuity, community-rooted vision and creative risk-taking can build institutions that last. Both began with limited resources and limitless ambition. Both chose access over elitism, dialogue over dogma. And both demonstrate the power of LeanSpark—purposeful simplicity, adaptive scalability, systemic sustainability and a relentless belief in lean execution.

These are not just cultural gatherings and experiments. They are movements. From shooting on an iPhone to winning an Oscar, that too is a movement. It is proof that simplicity, when executed with intent, can echo across the world.

<h1 style="text-align:center">2.2</h1>

Crafting a Career, Not Just a Résumé

Can LeanSpark Help You Build a Career?

Meet Sahiba and Surabhi, two young women, one from the cultural corridors of north India, the other from the policy trenches of the south. One thrives in front of the camera, the other behind the scenes in political backrooms. Their worlds couldn't be more different, and yet, their journeys echo the same core idea: when the system doesn't offer you a clear path, you create your own.

Sahiba Bali: Jill of Many Trades

Actor. Marketer. Content creator. Influencer. Lecturer. Media personality.

These are just a few of the many roles that Sahiba Bali has crammed into her barely decade-long career. Sahiba (born 1995) didn't inherit a legacy. She built one. No godfather, no industry surname, no viral debut. Just an ordinary Kashmiri girl raised in Delhi, navigating lecture halls by day and audition lines by evening.

A role in *Dear Zindagi* was her first toe-dip into cinema. No red carpet. Just sharp instincts, an unshakeable work ethic and a knack for telling stories that stick. What followed was a mosaic of moves: *Laila Majnu*, *Bard of Blood*, viral digital reels, marketing gigs, Shark Tank promos, even anchoring an IPL team.

This is Sahiba's story. Not of fame, but of refusing to choose one thing when you can be brilliant at five. Welcome to the world of multi-hyphenates. Sahiba Bali just happens to be one of its rockstars.

Bollywood Calling

A turning point in Sahiba Bali's journey came when Imtiaz Ali offered her a role in *Laila Majnu*. It felt like a dream. But there was a catch—she was in the UK, in the middle of completing her master's degree. Her parents weren't thrilled with the offer. 'It felt like a once-in-a-lifetime opportunity,' she says, 'but they were worried. I was supposed to be studying, not shooting a film in India.'

But Sahiba didn't pick one path over the other. She found a way to do both.

She shot the film while working on her dissertation. 'I did my thesis in Kashmir while we were shooting. There was no internet, so I carried all the books I needed from the UK. My luggage was so heavy, I had to pay extra at the airport,' she laughs. 'But somehow, working odd hours, I managed to pull it off.'

When she finally moved back to India, reality hit. Bollywood wasn't all lights and glamour. It was messy, unpredictable, often brutal. 'It's a scary place, to be honest,' she says. 'There are days when you're on set, and days when you're completely out of work.'

Sahiba's experience in Bollywood is a masterclass in Indian-style problem-solving—making things work, often with limited resources and a whole lot of creativity. She puts it simply: 'Jugaad is one of my favourite desi terms. I think it's very native to India, and I feel everyone here has some kind of jugaad skill.'

On film sets, this spirit showed up in countless ways. Shooting without formal permits is not unusual. What would be a legal hurdle abroad is often handled here with a 'let's do it until someone stops us' attitude. Crew members regularly double up as extras. A junior assistant director might step into a scene. A stylist might play a passer-by. It's all hands on deck.

Budgets are tight, schedules even tighter. Scenes meant to be shot at night are sometimes filmed in broad daylight and later altered in post-production. 'We'll fix it in the edit' becomes the default plan. VFX teams end up carrying the burden of last-minute improvisations.

But this isn't just about cutting corners. It's about making the best of what's available: precisely the LeanSpark way. Sahiba has literally lived by the approach. Whether it is figuring out how to finish a master's dissertation in the middle of a remote shoot or navigating the ever-shifting world of casting calls and film sets, she's constantly found her own way through.

Climbing up the Corporate Ladder

Sahiba Bali always knew she wanted to do both: act and work in the business world. With degrees in hand, she applied to companies like Grant Thornton and Paytm, but it was Zomato that changed the game for her.

She started in the corporate social responsibility (CSR) team, promoting Feeding India. With no marketing budget, she got creative. 'I'd worked on *Dangal* briefly and so I reached out to Sanya Malhotra and Fatima Shaikh, asking them to support the cause. It was good PR for them, and visibility for us.'

Her next move was Zomato Live, where she handled marketing for concerts and events. Here she mastered the art of bartering: VIP tickets and shoutouts in exchange for free products and stalls from small businesses. 'We didn't have big budgets, so we had to find smart ways to get things done.'

Eventually, she moved to brand marketing: leading campaigns and weaving Zomato into comedy shows and YouTube content. Here she was asked to launch the YouTube channel with zero budget. No money for influencers. No crew. Just her network and her hustle.

'I knew people in the industry because of my past work,' she says. 'So, I tapped into my contacts and cracked a loophole. During film promotions, production houses are open to brand collabs, often for free.'

So instead of reaching out to actors directly, Sahiba approached platforms like Amazon Prime instead. 'They were promoting a film called *Hiranya*. I told them, give us twenty minutes with the lead actor, and in return we'll plug your film on Zomato's platform.' That twenty-minute slot would've cost over ₹50 lakh otherwise. It worked. And she kept repeating the play, building a process around it.

She even brought in agencies like GroupM and Dentsu to scale the idea. Zomato's YouTube channel started featuring top stars, without spending crores. Her street-smart approach extended beyond content. Sahiba built gifting partnerships for Zomato Live events by bartering visibility for freebies like event stalls, celebrity mentions and social shoutouts.

What made her stand out was this blend of scrappiness, strategy and an insider's understanding of entertainment. She knew how to work the system: not to cut corners but navigate them smartly.

To Content Creation

Sahiba's career transition into content creation and her involvement with OTT platforms marks a significant chapter in her multifaceted journey. Her ability to seamlessly integrate her marketing background with her acting career has allowed her to create a unique personal brand on social media and explore new opportunities in the digital entertainment landscape.

The rise of OTT platforms has been a game changer in the entertainment industry, offering unprecedented flexibility and choice for viewers. Sahiba acknowledges this shift: 'With Netflix and Amazon you don't need to have big names to sell your content. It works by word of mouth.' This democratization of content has provided a platform for new talent to shine, offering opportunities for actors, writers and directors outside the traditional Bollywood circuit.

The Brand Called Sahiba

Sahiba Bali's marketing instincts continue to shape her work as a content creator. Back at Zomato, she realized early on that giving the right people perks like freebies, invites and backstage passes could unlock big visibility. That same mindset now guides her brand collaborations. She partners only with brands she genuinely believes in, keeping her content real and relatable.

In the process, her journey has expanded beyond solo projects. She's worked with platforms like FilterCopy and Dice Media, building a creative ecosystem of collaboration rather than competition.

In 2025, she took on a new role on Shark Tank India. 'I'm the new host,' she says with a smile. 'But it's not just about standing in front of the camera. The host's role is very brand-centric,' she explains. 'It requires me to tap into my business background to bridge storytelling with marketing.'

Influencers and creators are no longer just faces; they're full-fledged brands. 'Social media has democratized fame,' she says. And she's living proof of this.

Authenticity is a cornerstone of Sahiba's marketing approach. She wants to maintain a genuine connection with her audience through her endorsements and content. 'It is important to make sure that I believe in the brands I work with. I won't endorse something I don't personally use,' she says, emphasizing the trust that comes with authenticity.

Sahiba's journey may seem effortless but it carries its own weight. 'It's a huge mental and emotional burden,' she admits. Being in the public eye means constantly being 'on'. Social media doesn't help. 'If I shoot with a male actor, people start pairing us up. Even a friendly dinner can spiral into dating rumours.'

Instead of letting all this wear her down, she turns it into momentum. Her projects feed into each other. 'It's a win-win,' she says, using acting shoots to generate YouTube content, blending workstreams that others might keep separate.

The Blueprint Is Hers

Sahiba Bali knows exactly where she's headed, and just as importantly, where she's not. 'I know what I don't want to do: TV shows or reality shows,' she says, choosing projects that challenge her as an actor and reflect her range. Her goal is clear: to be an intelligent entertainer, someone respected not just for performance, but for perspective.

That's the LeanSpark philosophy in action: working with purpose, adapting with agility, and delivering impact without waste. Juggling corporate gigs, acting roles and now hosting Shark Tank. It's a lot. She is a 'Jill of all Trades'—one who's mastering the art of doing many things well.

The blueprint isn't borrowed. It's hers.

Surabhi Hodigere: Grit, Grace and 'Adjust Maadi'

She didn't grow up in a political dynasty. No last name that opened doors. Just a teenage girl with questions. At seventeen, Surabhi Hodigere walked into the world of Indian politics with burning curiosity and a borrowed pass to the Vidhana Soudha (the Karnataka Legislative Assembly). What started as an internship turned into a calling. And over the years, that calling has shaped a career that defies easy labels. Surabhi isn't just a policy wonk or a politician. She's a builder of narratives that challenge the status quo.

She was the youngest in the room. Often the only woman. 'Everyone else had some legacy. 'I had a laptop and conviction,' she laughs.

Losses and setbacks came early. Giving up was not an option. 'In Bangalore, we say *adjust maadi*,' she says. 'That's our instinct to stretch, flex, figure things out. I didn't know it back then, but it's the only reason I have survived this journey.'

For this Harvard Kennedy School graduate, LeanSpark is not just an approach, it is muscle memory. A way of life. She's not waiting for the system to change, she's challenging it.

Early Life and Influences

Surabhi's journey began with a personal loss. Her father passed away when she was just ten. That grief, she says, became fuel for her: 'A lot of my work has been driven by that loss.' Raised by a resilient mother, Surabhi grew up watching the strength it takes to rebuild a life. That early experience taught her the importance of making the most of what you have: a mindset that would later shape her political path.

At seventeen, she joined an election campaign to simply observe how things were done. 'I couldn't vote or contribute much, but I wanted to understand how it all worked.' By nineteen, she was interning with Krishna Byregowda, then a member of the Karnataka Legislative Assembly. This gave her a ringside view of how his office managed local grievances: everything from domestic violence cases to garbage complaints. That experience was eye-opening. 'I realized I wanted to be remembered as someone who came in and did something.'

But politics, she quickly figured, wasn't designed for women like her. 'I always wanted to push boundaries,' she says. But she found herself in spaces where men dominated conversations, and women, especially during campaigns, retreated to the kitchen. That struck a nerve. She wanted to change that too. Not just by showing up, but by making space for more women to see themselves as political actors.

An Entrepreneurial Approach

'I started a company mostly because my family said I couldn't be in politics,' Surabhi jokes. After an internship at nineteen, Surabhi knew she wanted to drive real change. But without political lineage or a recognizable surname, doors didn't open easily.

So, she launched Political Quotient, a firm that helps politicians and policymakers navigate governance using data and tech. 'I had to find a way to do politics, but also make money and make it look respectable,' she laughs. But behind the humour is grit. 'I'm very stubborn about doing what I want. I always have been.'

Political Quotient introduced tools like Smart Office, a tech solution for grievance redressal. It helped MLAs craft sharper legislative agendas. One friend gave her a piece of advice that stuck: 'If you're not using tech, you're not scaling.'

Surabhi doubled down on building lightweight, tech-driven solutions for better governance. One MLA reluctantly tried her system. Complaints that had taken weeks to process got tracked and resolved within days. Citizens noticed, politicians got praise, the word spread.

That was Surabhi's LeanSpark moment of using code and hustle to fix what power and protocol couldn't. A digitized complaint system and dashboard working together nudged the machinery of governance to function better for the people it was meant to serve. But the real friction wasn't just technical. It was cultural. Being a young woman in politics came with its own baggage.

The Harvard Experience

Surabhi's decision to go to Harvard wasn't just for the degree. It was about proving something to herself and to others. 'Coming from a non-political family, I needed something to fall back on,' she says. Harvard gave her not just knowledge, but credibility.

At Harvard Kennedy School she studied how governments use technology to serve people better. There she worked closely with digital governance expert David Eaves and dived deep into how digital public infrastructure (DPI) like Aadhaar and the Unified Payments Interface (UPI) worked. 'I always knew *what* I wanted to do. Harvard helped me figure out *how*.'

Surabhi's time at Harvard helped her connect the dots between technology, governance and people. She saw how data could drive better decisions and how digital tools could make governments more transparent. 'The tech part is easy,' she says. 'It's getting people to change that's hard.'

One of her biggest learnings was to 'listen more'. Being around students from different countries gave her the power of perspective. 'Half of finding solutions is hearing voices you don't usually hear,' she says, a lesson she carried back with her to India.

At home, she now had fresh ideas but faced the same old system. Running for elections, she realized, wasn't about good ideas or hard work, it was about money. Lots of it. 'When even the finance minister says she can't afford to contest elections, what hope does someone like me have?' she asks with a smile.

Surabhi's time at Harvard strengthened her belief that Indian politics needed more women. Not just as token candidates, but as decision-makers. She started the Naari Shakti Collective, a volunteer-driven group that trains and supports women who want to enter politics in Karnataka.

The process began with asking simple questions. Why aren't more women stepping up? What is holding them back?

She heard stories of fear, self-doubt and feeling alone. So Naari Shakti set out to build what was missing: practical workshops on public speaking, campaigning and digital tools; mentorship from experienced women leaders; and, most importantly, a safe space to talk, share and grow. Slowly, women began showing up. 'We focus on building confidence and providing practical training for women who want to enter politics,' she says. The collective aims not only to increase representation but also to foster an environment where women feel empowered to voice their opinions and influence policy.

Joining a Political Party

Surabhi Hodigere's current role as a spokesperson for the BJP marks a new phase in her political journey. After Harvard, she stepped into the spotlight, speaking on behalf of the party, explaining its vision and engaging with issues that matter to people.

'The way political parties work is mind-blowing,' she says. The chaos, the pace, the constant negotiation—it was a steep learning curve. But she soon found her footing, using her background in tech and governance to bring fresh ideas into policy conversations.

Her role as spokesperson isn't just about speaking—it's about listening. Talking to people, understanding their concerns and finding out how to drive change. 'Every day, I ask myself what kind of change I want to create and how to find the resources to make this happen,' she says.

In addition to her role in the BJP, Surabhi actively consults with start-ups that focus on technology policy and governance frameworks. This greater engagement enables her to stay at the forefront of innovation while contributing to the broader discourse on public policy. 'I consult with a few start-ups, particularly in the space sector, where we see a lot of innovation happening right now,' she says.

Her consulting work also often revolves around developing DPI and digital public goods (DPG), areas she became passionate about during her time at Harvard. 'It was in my blood to use technology for scale for every problem,' she explains, referring to how her academic experiences shaped her professional pursuits.

Surabhi's work reflects the core LeanSpark principle of adaptive scalability. This guides her work with start-ups, helping them navigate the messy realities of implementing tech solutions in slow-moving, bureaucratic systems.

The Grace behind the Grind

LeanSpark isn't just about fixing broken systems. It's a mindset. A quiet philosophy. One that says: work with what you have, act with purpose and don't wait for perfect conditions to begin. Surabhi sees echoes of this in Indian philosophy. 'You're dealt certain cards,' she says. 'You can choose what to do with them.'

Many religions have contemplated this dilemma. The idea of accepting your circumstances and moving forward with action resonates with the Bhagavad Gita's lesson of doing your duty without thinking of the results.

Jainism's *anekantavada* preaches that problems can be approached from many angles, and we must stay open to different paths. And Buddhism's *upaya* addresses being skilful with what's at hand. Even Stoic philosophy echoes this mindset. Marcus Aurelius wrote: 'What stands in the way becomes the way.'

In a world that prizes control and perfection, LeanSpark offers something different: grace in the face of uncertainty. A belief that progress can be imperfect.

That is how Surabhi lives.

* * *

Sahiba and Surabhi didn't wait for the perfect brief, the ideal role or a smooth runway. Their journeys show that LeanSpark isn't just for entrepreneurs or companies, it's for anyone crafting a life with intent.

Are you ready to build not just a résumé, but a life with spark?

2.3

Designing the Runway

Before Take-Off Comes the Ground Beneath

Some entrepreneurs build start-ups. Others build the space in which start-ups can grow. Manoj Kumar and Rajesh Nair are two ecosystem builders who are cultivating the landscape of Indian innovation. Manoj, through Social Alpha, has created a launchpad for entrepreneurs to solve hard, tech-heavy problems that the market alone can't address. Rajesh Nair works further upstream at the level of mindset, mentoring student innovators and catalysing grassroots ingenuity. Between them lies a powerful lesson: we need a meaningful ecosystem of innovation. Can we build these highways even while we are driving?

Social Alpha's Tryst with Innovators

For Manoj Kumar, jugaad isn't a shortcut. It's a mindset. He rejects it when it means 'quick fix', 'workaround', 'poor quality'. He embraces it when it stands for ingenuity and resourcefulness.

That's the philosophy of his company Social Alpha. Since 2016, it has backed over 300 start-ups that are solving hard problems through science and technology. The firm provides access to labs, incubators, seed funding and support with product development, business models and regulation.

Social Alpha isn't just an incubator. It's a launchpad for the kind of entrepreneurship India needs: high-impact and deeply rooted in purpose. This chapter looks at how he and his firm are helping entrepreneurs build solutions that are lean, scalable and designed for lasting impact.

Three Phases, One Mission

Before founding Social Alpha, Manoj Kumar wore many hats: CEO, investor and board member across the US, Europe and India. Banking, capital markets, venture capital, strategy—you name it, and he did it. In 2016, he stepped away from it all. Since then, he has focused on one thing: backing science and tech entrepreneurs who want to solve real problems for India and the world.

At the heart of his work is a deep insight into how India's entrepreneurial journey has evolved.

The first phase was all about services. Think Infosys. Companies that are running global operations with little capital and without access to venture funds, apps or the internet. Just smart use of talent to build sustainable businesses through IT services, BPO and analytics. It was lean, clever and home-grown.

The second phase came with the internet boom. Smartphones, apps, high-speed data and a new wave of start-ups emerged. Ola, Zomato, Flipkart. Venture capital poured in. Many of these ideas mirrored global models: Uber for Ola, Airbnb for Oyo. Some were uniquely Indian, too, like Bharat Matrimony. Most of these were service platforms. Few built core products.

And that's the problem, says Manoj. 'We built airline companies, not aircraft. We mastered IT services, not search engines or semiconductors. We've been a service economy, not a product one.' Because building products needs time, capital and risk. And India as a country hasn't invested enough in all this.

'To create a Flipkart, you don't need five years of R&D. But to build a medical device, you do,' Manoj says. You need to prototype, test, run clinical trials, get approvals and refine everything endlessly. All this takes time. Most start-ups don't have the patient capital or ecosystem to make that happen.

But what if the spirit of 'resourcefulness under constraint' were channelled through science and structure? 'What if a Tesla-like company used jugaad, not to cut corners, but to cut costs without compromising quality? What if an MRI machine from India could compete with GE, not just in price, but in performance?' asks Manoj.

That, he says, is the real potential. That's LeanSpark.

This needs a different kind of capital. Not the $200 million R&D budgets of the West, but what Manoj calls 'good enough capital': $10 million, say, over five years. Enough to prototype, test, iterate and ship world-class products built for real-world needs.

This, he says, is the third phase. The rise of deep tech and hardware start-ups in India. Backed by innovation, patient capital and bold entrepreneurs. This is what Social Alpha is doing.

From drones for farmers to affordable medical devices: The company is betting on founders who are willing to take the long road to success, not the quick exit. It's a new model of entrepreneurship, one that doesn't simply mimic the Silicon Valley playbook.

Playbook for Indian Ventures

Manoj Kumar uses a simple 2x2 matrix to explain his logic: One axis is risk; the other is return. While traditional venture capitalists (VCs) chase predictable returns, Manoj is betting on high-risk, long-term, science-led ventures. The reason is simple: India can build world-class products at a fraction of global R&D costs, $10 million vs $200 million, all with talent and lean execution.

He gives the example of Phool, a start-up from IIT Kanpur. The team has developed Fleather, a leather-like biomaterial made from fungi, in just five years. What would have cost millions elsewhere was done frugally in India. Phool raised venture capital only after many years of bootstrapping.

Unlike apps, product start-ups bleed cash early and can't follow the typical Series A to E route. Building a new TB vaccine or an electric battery isn't like building the next food delivery app. It takes time, science and endurance.

For Manoj, this is LeanSpark. It's not jugaad as a quick fix, but as a blend of deep tech, Indian business instinct and long-term thinking.

The *Product Entrepreneur* Mindset

Product entrepreneurs are wired differently. They're not chasing valuation. They're chasing real-world solutions.

Manoj sees three defining traits:

High Risk Appetite: Product entrepreneurs know VC money doesn't come easy. So, they bootstrap on grants, prize money and Department of Science and Technology (DST) schemes. Many start with just ₹10–20 lakh. Few have even raised a crore when they reach Social Alpha.

Hands-On and Technical: These entrepreneurs aren't B-school grads. They're engineers, scientists and medics: people who've worked in labs, not just on Excel. They build prototypes, not pitch decks. Founders of start-ups like Vidcare and Voxelgrids solder wires, test machines and write code.

Lean Execution: These entrepreneurs work from modest facilities, often self-built. Manoj recalls starting R&D for a new type of MRI machine in a spare bedroom. No million-dollar labs. Just grit. MIT and Boston start-ups might have plush set-ups. Here, ₹50 lakh from the government is often delayed and another ₹50 lakh from Social Alpha is what keeps things going.

Add to this the vital ingredient of resilience. Many of the entrepreneurs Manoj supports sell their assets, borrow money and still push forward. They don't quit. They iterate and endure. And that's what reminds Manoj of founders like Steve

Jobs and Elon Musk, not because they're rich and famous, but because they slept on the floors of factories and put everything they had into building something that matters.

The Scaling Story

How do you scale in such an environment? Once the prototype for a vaccine, diagnostic tool or device is built, the game changes. Now you need capital, regulators, partners and distribution networks. You need to work with the Indian Council of Medical Research (ICMR), the World Health Organization (WHO) or government procurement systems. This is where start-ups have to partner with large players.

One of Manoj's ventures was acquired by Reliance. Jio now takes care of distribution—because scaling a product isn't the same as building it. In agri-tech, small start-ups can't afford their own sales teams. So Social Alpha works with Farmer Producer Organizations (FPOs) in UP and Odisha, training them to become low-cost distributors. It's still frugal but it is also clever. And always trying to find a way in and out.

Protecting IP, Even When You Build Lean

One of the biggest myths about lean solutions is that they can't be protected. That they are 'chalu' and temporary. But that's far from the truth. At Social Alpha, all new ventures are encouraged to file for IP from day one. This starts in India, then expands globally. The logic is simple: if your innovation solves a real problem, it deserves to be protected. Even if you built it with limited capital.

Pharma companies in the West charge high prices because of massive R&D spends. But what if you created a breakthrough product for a fraction of that cost? Could you still monetize it? Yes, but only if you own the IP behind it.

Frugal founders often create breakthrough products with limited capital. But that doesn't mean they compromise on standards. Many of Social Alpha's start-ups file patents, meet global biosafety norms and even secure FDA approvals. They're not cutting corners, they're cutting waste.

As Manoj puts it, 'Jugaad isn't the absence of rigour—it's the smart use of resources without skipping standards.' And protection is part of that rigour. Every solution that solves a real problem deserves IP protection. LeanSpark innovation means building high-quality products with discipline, under constraint, and then securing their value for the long haul.

VoxelGrids: Building an MRI from a Bedroom

Arjun Arunachalam, an IIT Bombay graduate with a PhD in imaging physics, had a bold idea to build a low-cost MRI machine without using liquid helium. Working in the US with GE, he knew MRI machines were expensive because of helium-cooled magnets. What if the magnet could be replaced altogether?

No one wanted to fund him. Until he met Manoj, who was just setting up Social Alpha then. Without a big cheque to offer, Manoj gave Arjun a desk, support and belief.

The work began in Manoj's apartment. Arjun sourced a magnet from Boston, wrote AI-based reconstruction algorithms, and slowly, piece by piece, built the machine. A hospital in Bangalore lent them their radiology space. Just as testing began, COVID hit. With hospitals shut down, they couldn't conduct clinical trials, but that's when the big players like GE, Siemens and Philips took notice.

Then came an even bigger surprise: Philips made an acquisition offer. Arjun and Manoj held off. With just days left to decide on Philips' offer, another breakthrough materialized. Zoho Corporation, excited by the project's potential, offered $5 million in funding, giving VoxelGrids a three-year runway. With this, they started clinical trials and later received regulatory approval from the Central Drugs Standard Control Organisation (CDSCO), India's equivalent of the US Food & Drug Administration (FDA). The team was now set to manufacture and sell the MRI machine, with plans for FDA approval soon.

Today, VoxelGrids is manufacturing MRI machines, competing with GE, Siemens and Philips, but built with less than $10 million over eight years.

VoxelGrids' journey proves what LeanSpark stands for. With the right mix of lean execution and strategic partnerships, it's possible to build cutting-edge products with minimal resources. Their story is about purposeful simplicity which cuts out unnecessary complexity to keep the product affordable and functional. It also reflects systemic sustainability which reduces long-term costs and reliance on foreign technologies. This is a blueprint for building world-class products in India and on India's terms.

Building the Road While Driving

'When we adopted the Silicon Valley model in India,' says Manoj, 'it worked. We built companies like Flipkart, Ola and Zomato, proving that this approach can succeed in India. However, none of them are high-tech research start-ups, and that's the missing piece. The US has had institutions like DARPA (Defense Advanced Research Projects Agency) for years, funding high-risk innovations like the internet and the mRNA platform.

'In the US and Europe, specialized institutions handle R&D, incubation and deployment. But in India, we have to build the entire system ourselves. It's like Tesla building its own charging stations and standards, or Google creating Android. When you're a pioneer, you have to build the whole ecosystem from scratch. We're building both highways and cars at the same time. Here's the good news; this means we can leapfrog old systems.'

As Manoj puts it, 'We're building infrastructure in parallel with the products. In places like Bangalore, we're developing Electronic City, Whitefield and attracting international investors, all while constructing a metro system.'

The real innovation isn't just in the products, though; it's in the mindset. India's entrepreneurs have shown they can build with less. What they need now is an ecosystem that believes in them just as much. That's what Social Alpha is for: a bridge between ambition and access, between frugality and scale. This is not just about solving for India. It's about showing the world how to build better with less, for more.

Rajesh Nair: The Spark Maker

In a village in Kerala, a young boy sat transfixed, ears pressed to a transistor radio, his only window to the outside world. Music floated out of the little box, and Rajesh Nair had a theory.

'There must be tiny people inside,' he thought. 'And when you turn the knob, they just sing louder.'

One day, unable to resist, he took the radio to a local repair shop and asked them to open it. What he saw amazed him. No tiny people, just coils, capacitors and wires. The technician showed him how radio waves worked, and even how to build a crystal radio himself. That single moment cracked open a new universe. 'If not for that encounter,' Rajesh says now, 'I'd probably have become a government official somewhere in provincial India.'

He studied physics and electrical engineering at the Indian Institute of Science, Bangalore. He then headed to the University of Massachusetts to specialize in manufacturing engineering. 'I wanted to design electronics,' he says. 'But to design well, you need to understand how things are made.'

Rajesh went on to design over 150 electromechanical products for Apple, GE and IBM. He didn't just work for the giants, though. He also built four of his own companies from scratch. Somewhere along the way, however, all this success left him with questions. After what he calls a 'midlife crisis', he ended up at the Massachusetts Institute of Technology (MIT) to study systems design and management. And to rediscover that boy who believed in little people inside radios.

This is Rajesh's journey. A story of taking things apart, be it radios, companies or ideas, and putting them back together with greater clarity and purpose.

The MIT Moment

At MIT, Rajesh received a fellowship from Ratan Tata that paid for his field work. This took him all over the world: deep into villages with tribal communities, places where people had never heard the word 'innovation' and yet practised it daily. He saw frugal hacks, ingenious tools and clever solutions to everyday problems. What struck him wasn't the lack of creativity, it was the lack of support.

'Innovation was very deep and innate among these people,' he says. 'But they didn't have the ability to duplicate or scale their ideas.' That's when his mission sharpened. He didn't just want to build products anymore; he wanted to build creators and entrepreneurs.

Rajesh began working with students, especially those from disadvantaged backgrounds, and developed a powerful model to guide their transformation: the zero–maker–innovator–entrepreneur pathway.

Zero to maker was the first leap: from no experience to hands-on creation. Rajesh used digital fabrication tools to help students build real products in just two days. Confidence was the key. 'You take someone uninitiated,' he says, 'and teach them how to learn by doing.'

Then came the innovator stage: where students identified problems, evaluated impact and built solutions. A simplified version of design thinking formed the backbone, structured enough to guide, but loose enough to spark originality.

Finally, the entrepreneur phase: turning ideas into ventures, and problems into opportunities. Students learnt to find customers, test value propositions and build sustainable models, even at a young age.

'The best time to engage people,' he insists, 'is in early middle school. By college, their thinking has settled or calcified. We need to reach the child before school kills creativity.'

His workshops have since reached thousands. The impact isn't just in the prototypes built, but in the identities forged. The boy who believed there were little people singing inside a radio now spends his time awakening makers and innovators in places most others overlook.

Lessons from the World

Over the years, Rajesh has taken his message far and wide. He has held over 125 workshops, across India, South Africa, Malaysia and the US. The setting may shift, but the spark he's looking to ignite remains the same: how to turn resourceful minds into resilient doers.

And through this whirlwind of classrooms, maker labs and village halls, Rajesh has gathered a few truths.

It's all about exposure. 'What's the biggest difference between a child in a private school in Delhi and one in a tribal school in Jharkhand?' Rajesh asks. 'It's not intelligence. It's exposure.' His belief is radical in its simplicity: entrepreneurship doesn't begin at twenty. It begins at ten. If we want a generation of job creators, we need to reach them before school squeezes out the sense of wonder from them.

Confidence is the first casualty of bias. In almost every workshop he does, he sees this: the girls hesitate. They doubt themselves. Social expectations whisper, 'This isn't for you.' But give them a few days, the right tools and the space to fail safely, and their confidence levels shoot up. Soon it matches that of the boys. 'It's not ability we need to fix. It's belief.'

Teachers need unlearning too. One of the toughest nuts to crack is the mindset of the teachers. Many see hands-on making as 'unacademic'. Others feel threatened by what they don't know. Rajesh urges them to learn alongside their students. 'When teachers become vulnerable,' he says, 'the classroom comes alive.'

Innovation needs ecosystems. Rajesh builds vibrant spaces filled with tools, mentors, peers and the permission to tinker. Think 'maker spaces': tinkering labs that are 'the playgrounds of innovation'. These aren't on elite campuses. They're often in rural areas, yet they pulse with possibility.

And at the heart of it all? The mindset of frugal ingenuity.

Rajesh calls this 'the beginning of the innovation process'. It's what happens when people have nothing but try anyway. For example, when working with Apple on thermal designs for the iPad and MacBook Air, his own company created a low-cost solution using PVC pipes and water to measure airflow, a jugaad approach that worked when Apple's simulations were insufficient.

To him, this mindset is a gateway drug to innovation that is messy, hands-on and full of friction. It thrives on constraints. 'A local village schoolkid can out-innovate an engineering topper. Because they've failed more, built more and guessed less,' says Rajesh.

Ecosystems are needed to support this mindset. That's where LeanSpark comes in, taking the instinctive energy of ingenuity and giving it form, structure and momentum. 'A mouse can't scale to be an elephant,' Rajesh reminds us, 'but with the right ecosystem and support, it can still punch above its weight.'

Centre, Community and Culture

To scale the LeanSpark mindset into something enduring, Rajesh believes we need more than tools. His ecosystem model rests on three pillars: centre, community and culture. The centre is the physical space, filled with tools, materials and resources. The community brings together learners, mentors and facilitators. But the most vital piece is culture. A living, breathing spirit of experimentation passed from one cohort to the next. 'At MIT,' he explains, 'students leave every few years, but the culture stays. That's what keeps innovation alive.'

Rajesh has built maker labs across Southeast Asia and beyond, but he's seen many fail when they focused only on shiny infrastructure. Referencing Josh Lerner's book *Boulevard of Broken Dreams*, Rajesh sees that many institutions 'have set up these centres without the community and culture, and they have failed.'

Without mentorship, without community, without the culture of grit and playful failure, everything collapses. That's why his programmes train university students to become mentors for schoolkids, creating regional innovation ecosystems from the bottom up.

In one such initiative, even unemployed youth built IoT devices and robots in schools that didn't have computers or internet. The secret is the culture that embraces failure as part of learning.

'An entrepreneur never fails,' he says. 'The project might. But failure is just tuition.' This approach rooted in frugality, experimentation and community is about creating systemic sustainability. Building systems that support ingenuity at scale, lighting sparks that don't just flicker, but sustain.

Changing Mindsets, Scaling Impact

Rajesh Nair has seen first-hand how little ingenious innovations can light up lives. He also knows that such innovations face an image problem. The words 'frugal' and 'jugaad' often carry baggage. They are seen as a shortcut, a compromise, something that's clever but not good enough. Rajesh wants to change that. 'The meaning of jugaad as low quality has to change,' he says. While in India the word is sometimes dismissed, he points out that in the West, it's celebrated. 'There, they don't know the Hindi meaning, but no one has a problem using the word and concept to create things.'

We have to stop seeing frugal as cheap, and start seeing it as constraint-driven innovation. It's about thinking smarter when you don't have everything you need.

People often worry that this kind of frugal thinking cuts corners. Rajesh agrees it's a risk, but not an inevitability. 'Every innovation requires constraint,' he says. That doesn't mean poor quality. It means going back to the fundamentals of purposeful simplicity. What really matters and what you can redesign.

That's the heart of LeanSpark: not cutting corners but carving out clarity.

* * *

This is what real culture-building looks like: not just launching start-ups, but nurturing ecosystems. Manoj builds bridges between science and society. Rajesh ignites minds that never saw themselves as innovators. One builds capital infrastructure; the other rewires cultural DNA. Together, they show that LeanSpark is a powerful mindset. And if India is to lead with innovation that's lean, purposeful and built to last, we need many more such ecosystem builders.

2.4

From Boardroom to Blackboard

The '*Zid*' to Educate

Shaveta Sharma Kukreja grew up in two worlds. One, the security of a middle-class Indian home filled with bookshelves, good education and ambition. The other, a country swirling with contrasts: gleaming apartments versus overcrowded schools, and privilege brushing past poverty on every street corner. 'The haves and have-nots weren't abstract ideas,' she says. 'They lived right next to us.'

When she grew up, Shaveta did what many young Indians do: she went to IIM Bangalore, joined the corporate world and rose through the ranks. But something inside her kept whispering: this isn't it. When friends spoke of the social sector or impact, she didn't even have the vocabulary to respond.

Not until she met Ashish Dhawan just as he was launching the Central Square Foundation. 'Ashish's vision for CSF resonated deeply with me,' she says. 'It offered a platform to work on education, a sector that had personally impacted my life.'

This wasn't charity. This was systems change. This was education as an equalizer. A way to bridge her two worlds.

The Early Years at CSF

When the chance came to build something that could change how India learns, she couldn't walk away. CSF in 2012 wasn't a big institution, it was a huddle around a dining table. But it had vision, resources and urgency. 'We were a small team navigating a mammoth system,' she says. Government spending dominated the education sector. But CSF, under Ashish Dhawan's stewardship, dared to think long-term. It wasn't just about teaching better. It was about changing the system that decides *who* gets taught and *how*. Shaveta took her corporate toolkit of systems thinking, operational clarity and strategic execution, and applied it to a sector that often lacked exactly those skills.

When Ashish Dhawan launched CSF, he wasn't trying to build just another NGO, he was building a revolution. Inspired by his time at Harvard, and by the bold movements that shaped Asia, he imagined CSF as a sort of marketplace for ideas, a platform where change-makers could gather, exchange views and drive transformation in India's education system.

In its early days, CSF had hustle in its DNA. 'We had a three-pronged approach,' recalls Shaveta. 'We gave grants to promising ideas, we did research that was rooted in real problems and we tried to influence policy directly.' In short:

fund the doers, study what works and change the system from within.

Shaveta and the team zoomed in on four key areas:

Human Capital: Most of the government's education budget went into salaries, yet there was little focus on leadership or training. CSF set up the India School Leadership Institute to build capacity among principals and education officials.

Ed-Tech: Long before Zoom classrooms became the norm, CSF was supporting platforms like Chimple and Diksha. But it wasn't just about launching apps. It was about making sure these tools worked for the students who needed them most.

Assessments: If you can't measure it, you can't improve it. CSF pushed for better data on learning outcomes, measuring what kids were really learning, not just what the textbooks said they should be.

Affordable Private Schools: Despite government schools being free, many low-income families chose to pay for private ones, hoping for better quality. CSF didn't dismiss them; they stepped in to improve them.

Running through all of this is a unique approach. Shaveta notes that philanthropic spending in education is about 3 per cent relative to government spending. 'That means that NGOs can't go it alone. You can't change education in India unless you work with the government.' And so, CSF's guiding belief is to collaborate—influence from within, not from the sidelines.

The Provocation

In 2018, something shifted at CSF.

After five years of bold bets and early wins, the organization hit pause, not because things weren't working, but because they needed to work better. The catalyst was a nudge from Dr Pramath Raj Sinha, a member of CSF's advisory board. He posed the question no one else had asked: 'What exactly is your mission and is grant-making enough to get you there?'

Sinha's provocation came at a pivotal moment for CSF. During the previous five years, the organization had been operating primarily as a grant-making entity. Now his question about the sustainability and impact of this approach prompted CSF to reflect on its mission and how it could achieve more significant systemic reforms.

'Pramath's questions were a moment of reckoning,' says Shaveta. The team realized that writing cheques wasn't enough to truly move the needle on India's education crisis. The mission needed muscle. And that muscle came in the form of a powerful new partner: the Bill & Melinda Gates Foundation.

The new partnership wasn't just about more funding, though. It was about a mindset shift. With the Gates Foundation as its first country partner in India, CSF began to pivot from being a generalist grant-maker to becoming a sharper, more focused change-maker. The foundation moved to project funding, concentrating deeply on two high-impact areas: early learning, specifically foundational literacy and numeracy, and ed-tech.

'It was our growing-up moment,' says Shaveta. The work became more strategic, more embedded. CSF began working hand-in-hand with government bodies to co-create scalable programmes. The goal wasn't just innovation anymore. It was integration in the true spirit of systemic sustainability, the LeanSpark way.

Using Ed-Tech

CSF has been a pioneer in using technology to improve learning, long before digital tools became mainstream.

Chimple, an ed-tech company, was born when its founder, a techie, saw his security guard's daughter struggle with learning. He created a playful app to teach her English and maths using short, engaging games. CSF backed Chimple early on, recognizing its frugal yet powerful design. Research showed that just ten minutes of use a week could give kids the same learning gains as a full year in school. Schools run by the Bharti Foundation began adopting it, and during the pandemic, its usage exploded: proof that well-designed tools can close learning gaps even in low-resource settings.

Diksha, a national platform for teachers, supported by CSF and Google, is a similar case. Think of it as a digital highway where high-quality lessons, videos and teaching resources flow freely. But a highway is only useful if there's traffic, so CSF helped develop content and partnered with platforms like YouTube and TikTok to spread the word. During the lockdown, Diksha reached millions, with some states broadcasting its lessons on television.

These stories are embedded in the essence of purposeful simplicity and adaptive scalability: start small, build with purpose and scale through partnerships. CSF's approach shows how technology, used thoughtfully, can unlock opportunity at scale.

The Scaling Challenge

'Scaling innovations in the education sector,' says Shaveta, 'is fraught with challenges, from securing funding to navigating complex bureaucratic systems.' CSF faced these hurdles, yet it was able to make significant strides in mainstreaming innovative solutions.

Bureaucracy is often a major hurdle for non-government organizations (NGOs), especially smaller ones. Working with the government can be complex and slow but, as Shaveta puts it, 'No NGO can create a parallel structure to the government. The government is the most important stakeholder. Anyone working in this space realizes this immediately.'

The government's role goes beyond just funding. It also provides the infrastructure and policy environment needed to scale ideas. An example of this was the 2020 National Education Policy (NEP) which recognized early learning as a priority. This was a major win for NGOs pushing for better foundational learning.

CSF's model of scaling has always leaned on partnerships. By working with the government, NGOs and the private sector, they've been able to do far more than they could alone. This has helped CSF deepen its government engagement and refine its approach.

CSF's work in states like Uttar Pradesh and Madhya Pradesh shows how strong local partnerships matter. In UP, for example, CSF joined forces with a team in Lucknow to develop workbooks and daily lesson plans, which were then distributed by the state government. This kind of coalition-building is what allows ideas to take root and grow.

Build Boldly, Exit Gracefully

In education reform, quick wins are rare. What really matters is staying power. CSF has shown that lasting change comes from patience, persistence and the belief that small steps, taken consistently, can lead to big shifts.

Their work on the NIPUN Bharat (National Initiative for Proficiency in Reading with Understanding and Numeracy) mission reflects this philosophy. Shaveta puts it this way, 'For us, the most ambitious articulation is an exit strategy.' CSF doesn't want to run programmes forever. Their goal is to build smart, cost-effective solutions that the government can eventually own and scale.

That kind of scale doesn't come easy. It takes what Shaveta calls *zid*—stubborn determination. 'How come our kids can't read or do simple maths?' she asks. 'Okay, if there are no quick wins, I have my core DNA of persistence: *zid kar rahi hun.* I am being stubborn.' When results take time, it's this quiet insistence that keeps CSF going. Not a flashy kind of urgency, but a deep resolve to see things through.

And behind that resolve is trust. CSF's partnerships with governments are built on respect and empathy. They know the system is complex. But rather than work around it, they work with it.

NIPUN Bharat is a prime example of how persistence and strategic partnerships can lead to significant success. This mission aims to ensure that every child in grade three can read with meaning and perform basic maths operations. Initially, it was a response to the learning crisis highlighted by Annual Status of Education Report (ASER) surveys, which showed that more than 70 per cent of grade five children could not read a grade three text.

Shaveta notes that 'nothing becomes mainstream if the government doesn't adopt it'. The fact that NIPUN Bharat has become a national priority underscores the success of CSF's collaborative approach. The initiative's impact is also evident in ASER surveys which have shown an upward trend in learning outcomes for the first time. This progress is attributed to the collective efforts of civil society, government and NGOs working together to prioritize early learning.

Success isn't just about launching good programmes; systemic sustainability is knowing when to step back. Long-term impact means building something strong enough that the government can eventually run it on its own.

Shaheen Mistri's Teach for India

CSF's contribution to Indian education is significant, and it is part of a wider movement. Many other organizations are driving change in their own focused ways, often complementing each other across the ecosystem. One example is Teach for India (TFI).

By placing young leaders inside classrooms, TFI creates impact while also nurturing a generation of future education reformers. It's a different model but powered by the same belief: that change in education begins with bold ideas, grounded action and the patience to scale what sticks.

Shaheen Mistri's journey in Indian education began with a powerful realization: the stark contrast between the educational opportunities afforded to the privileged and those denied to the underprivileged. This realization ignited a passion to bridge the divide in India's educational system, sparking a movement that continues to grow and inspire.

In 1989, Mistri, who grew up in Mumbai, founded the Akanksha Foundation in her native city. Starting with a group of fifteen children in a modest educational centre, Mistri set out to provide more than just after-school tutoring. The foundation's initial focus was on English, maths, values and extracurricular activities. This eventually grew into a network of schools, offering a lifeline to thousands of children from low-income communities. Built on a foundation of LeanSpark, the Akanksha model cleverly harnessed community resources and the power of volunteers to keep costs low while achieving high impact, proving that change doesn't need to be expensive to be transformative.

In 2009, Mistri launched Teach for India to build a movement of young leaders who would commit to teaching in under-resourced schools. Like the American organization on which it is based, TFI recruits and trains young leaders to teach in under-resourced schools, aiming to provide quality education and inspire systemic change from the classroom up. Through its highly selective fellowship, TFI places passionate graduates and professionals in classrooms across India, with the vision that 'one day all children will attain an excellent education'.

Instead of building new schools or relying on fancy infrastructure, TFI works with what already exists. It uses government schools, taps into local resources and focuses on making the most of them. A model that's cost-effective, scalable and sustainable.

Since its start, TFI has helped over 5000 students in Mumbai, Pune and Delhi graduate from grade ten, often with better results than nearby government schools. In 2020, their fourth batch graduated with a pass rate of 94 per cent. Even in 2023, despite the challenges, 89 per cent of their students cleared grade ten. That's real, measurable impact right where it matters most.

To scale this vision, TFI built Firki, an online platform for teachers. It offers free courses, webinars and resources in multiple Indian languages, helping thousands of teachers across the country build skills at their own pace.

TFI also runs TFIx, an incubation programme that helps education entrepreneurs build their own local fellowships. It follows a simple, structured journey: build, launch and grow. Through mentorship, site visits and shared resources, TFIx allows leaders in different parts of the country to adapt and carry the model forward in their own communities.

All of this is supported by strong partnerships, with philanthropies like the Michael and Susan Dell Foundation, corporate sponsors and the global Teach for All network. This backing lets TFI stay agile and bold, investing in new ideas like Firki and TFIx.

The results speak for themselves. TFI students do better than peers in similar schools. Over 90 per cent of teaching fellows stay on in education after their two years, and alumni have already reached over 33 million children, through teaching, policy and social ventures.

What's more, TFI has used crowdsourcing to raise funds, showing that money doesn't have to be a barrier when communities believe in the cause. It's a model built on clarity of purpose, smart use of resources and trust in people.

A Quiet Revolution

CSF and TFI show us that transformation isn't always dramatic, it's deliberate. It's the result of staying the course, working with what's available and refusing to give up on what's essential, quite the LeanSpark way.

The two organizations have adopted different approaches, and yet they have the same compelling mission. TFI works from the ground up: building leaders inside classrooms, one child, one teacher, one community at a time. CSF works from the top down: shaping systems, aligning governments, embedding change into the DNA of education policy. One breathes life into learning at the grassroots. The other builds the scaffolding that holds it all up.

The future of education in India won't be powered by massive overhauls or billion-dollar bets. It will be built through coalitions of teachers, policymakers, entrepreneurs and dreamers, who know that even a broken system can be rebuilt if you start small, stay patient and never stop showing up.

It's a quiet revolution. And it has already begun.

Section III

LeanSpark Nation

Innovations Built to Scale

Whether it's building home-grown AI that speaks every Indian language, creating digital platforms that deliver welfare at scale, launching satellites on a shoestring budget or nurturing talent through sports, the chapters in this section show how India is quietly rewriting the rules of inclusive growth through frugal innovation. These stories prove that nation-building isn't just about big money or flashy tech but about designing systems that work for everyone.

We wanted to test a hunch: Could the LeanSpark mindset unlock excellence in sport too? Enter Nandan Kamath of GoSports. Always on the move and hard to get in touch with. So, we connected with Deepthi Bopaiah instead, who Mukesh met at a Peter Diamandis talk. Deepthi began our interview with a line she remembered from her first MBA class—one that still shapes how she thinks about talent, discipline and ambition. We knew right away: her story belonged in the book.

Then there's Vivek Raghavan, Jaideep's IIT batchmate and long-time friend. From the Unique Identification Authority of India (UIDAI) to India's AI mission, Vivek has been at the heart of India's boldest digital experiments. He's a regular speaker in our Ashoka classroom. Through him we explored what it means to build *at scale* for 1.4 billion people while staying true to first principles.

Nandan Nilekani's contribution to nation-building had to feature in this section. Jaideep has interviewed him several times over the years. The Aadhaar story, and its seismic effects on Indian governance, financial inclusion and digital infrastructure remains one of the most audacious LeanSpark feats in contemporary India and the world.

What about space, then? That chapter is inspired by a special session with Prof. Somak Raychaudhury, vice chancellor of Ashoka University and a noted astrophysicist who has advised ISRO. We paired him with Jaideep for a *jugalbandi* with our students. From Mars missions on frugal budgets to a blend of jugaad and structured innovation, that session pushed us to explore the elements of LeanSpark in India's space story. It was the perfect finale.

These aren't just national achievements. They are signs that India is building with courage despite constraints.

LeanSpark is not just a mindset for start-ups or social impact. It's also a framework for how we govern and dream at scale as a nation.

3.1

India's Sporting Grit

Going for Gold

'The only thing you need to know in life is jugaad,' said Professor Kamath on Deepthi Bopaiah's first day at Symbiosis Institute of Management Studies (SIMS) in Pune. And then, rather than lecturing his new students on the concept, he put them to the test. He instructed the class to leave behind all their possessions—cash, cards and other resources—and said, 'Your challenge today is to venture out into the city and earn money by the end of the day.'

'Many of us were in Pune for the first time,' Deepthi recalls, the shock of that moment still fresh in her mind.

The students were divided into groups and assigned to different parts of the city. Deepthi's group was sent to Koregaon Park, a bustling neighbourhood known for its upscale restaurants and shops.

As they set out, the reality of the task before them began to sink in. How would they navigate the city without transportation? How would they convince strangers to give them work without any credentials or references? This was a crash course in resilience and creative problem-solving.

The challenge pushed Deepthi and her classmates to their limits, forcing them to rely on their wits and innate resourcefulness. By the end of the day, Deepthi had managed to secure two jobs: one at a garment store and another at a restaurant.

At the garment store, she sold clothes, drawing on a hitherto hidden ability to persuade customers to try on things and pay for them. In the restaurant, she assisted with serving the clientele, showcasing her interpersonal abilities. 'It was amazing,' she says, 'because I had to draw on all these life skills I didn't realize I had. When push came to shove, I just had to figure out what I could do.'

In the evening, the class reconvened to discuss their experiences. In the debriefing session, they reflected on what had worked and what hadn't, why some had succeeded while others had faltered. 'It became clear that success in this challenge—as in life—often came down to your ability to think on your feet, communicate effectively and persist in the face of adversity.'

This challenge brought home to Deepthi the importance of being able to step out of her comfort zone and open herself up to failure and rejection. Some students excelled, finding multiple jobs and even receiving offers for permanent positions. Others struggled, unable to overcome their hesitation to ask for help or opportunities. 'That contrast was very interesting,' she says. 'How, at the end of the day, some of us had two jobs, and had made money, while others didn't even leave the campus, because they had thought: How am I going to ask anyone for a lift, or how will I even get to where I have to be?'

For Deepthi, the experience would serve as a very real lesson in the practical application of LeanSpark. 'I realized then,' she says, 'that jugaad isn't about cutting corners or finding easy solutions, but rather about leveraging creativity and resourcefulness to overcome constraints.'

In the high-performance world of sports, success is often seen as a function of big budgets, elite infrastructure and global exposure. But in India, where talent far outpaces access, a different kind of playbook is emerging—one powered by the LeanSpark mindset. Deepthi's journey from a resource-challenged MBA exercise in Koregaon Park to building systems of support for India's athletes through GoSports Foundation, is a living testament to this philosophy. In this chapter we explore her story that shows innovation in sport doesn't always require stadiums and sponsorships. Sometimes it starts with a simple question: What can we do with what we already have?

From HSBC to GoSports Foundation

In 2012, as India grappled with its Olympic performance in London, Deepthi found herself at a crossroads. Secure at HSBC in a high-paying job, she couldn't ignore the growing restlessness within. 'Everyone was talking about how India was underperforming in sports. I felt like I had to be part of the solution,' she recalls.

Around that time, she came across GoSports Foundation through friends. Their mission—to back India's sporting talent—struck a chord. That same year, she took the plunge, leaving behind corporate comfort to join the nonprofit.

'When I joined, we supported just fourteen to fifteen athletes and struggled to raise ₹25 lakh a year,' she says. 'Now, we support 200 athletes, run five academies and raise nearly ₹40 crore annually.'

Looking back, she calls it the best decision of her life. 'To see the mindset of champions up close, to help them reach global podiums—this is nation-building. Every anthem we hear at an international event makes everything worthwhile.'

Leading through the Labyrinth

Over the years, Deepthi's role at GoSports Foundation evolved steadily from supporter to strategist, from programme builder to visionary. Today, she serves as the CEO, guiding the foundation through some of the toughest terrains in Indian sport. Her leadership has been marked not just by scaling the organization's reach, but by squarely confronting the deeper structural issues that hinder athlete development across the country. While the job has been fulfilling, it has also been anything but easy.

Indian sport faces two major hurdles: resource constraints and cultural-systemic barriers. As Deepthi says, 'People don't have access to training, to equipment, to nutrition, to shoes, to competitions.' This lack of support results in a staggering 70–75 per cent athlete dropout rate at the national level. While funding exists for elite performers, the system neglects the broader talent pool. 'We're funding the top 200 athletes. But we should be focusing on the next 2000,' she says.

The second challenge is mindset. Sport is often seen as non-essential, overshadowed by causes like education or employment. 'Why should we give to sport, potential supporters ask, when there are so many basic issues like education, women's welfare and youth development. This perception, combined with fragmented governance, makes sustained progress difficult. With sport being a state subject, investment varies widely. While some states offer generous rewards for medallists, most typically underinvest in long-term preparation,' says Deepthi.

Odisha is a rare success story, where vision, investment and public–private partnerships have transformed hockey. Bopaiah sees this as the model to push for, where support comes early, not just when the medals arrive.

GoSports Foundation's Approach

Faced with deep-rooted constraints in sports, the foundation has pioneered innovations that create big impact without big budgets. Rather than replicating expensive international models, GoSports has focused on four key levers to spark sustainable change:

Smart Scholarships, not Blank Cheques: One of GoSports Foundation's most impactful innovations is its scholarship model, which reimagines how talent is identified and supported in India. Instead of relying on expensive and often exclusive talent scouting methods, the foundation invites athletes to apply for scholarships—making the process aspirational, inclusive and self-driven. 'You have to apply for our scholarship,' says Deepthi Bopaiah. 'And we say to our athletes: You're a

GoSports scholar, and you will be a scholar for the rest of your life.' This model, while cutting down the costs and biases of traditional scouting, also empowers athletes to take ownership of their careers.

By reimagining the funding model through a LeanSpark lens—targeted, scalable and demand-led, GoSports has built a system where talent doesn't have to chase visibility. Instead, opportunity becomes something to apply for, not just to hope for.

Building a Sports Ecosystem on a Budget: Building a robust sports ecosystem requires strategic planning and resourcefulness, especially when operating on a budget. GoSports Foundation has excelled in creating an ecosystem that supports athletes' holistic development. The foundation's focus is not just on immediate results but on building long-term pathways for athletic success. By addressing dropout rates and providing sustained support, GoSports ensures that talented athletes have the resources they need to progress in their careers.

Leveraging Partnerships and CSR Funding: Partnerships and CSR play a vital role in GoSports Foundation's operations. The foundation has successfully partnered with several corporations to secure funding for its programmes. 'We are very unique because we do programmes so a particular corporate can own the entire programme,' she explains.

The CSR law in India has been instrumental in channelling funds towards sports development. '2013 was a turning point because when the CSR law came into India, it actually had a category of training towards Paralympics and rural sport,'

Deepthi highlights. By aligning corporate interests with sports initiatives, GoSports has been able to secure sustained funding from major corporations like the Infosys Foundation and others.

Besides provide financial support, these partnerships also help build an ecosystem where corporates are actively involved in athlete development. 'We are probably among the top two organizations that actually get the majority of the CSR funding that comes to sport,' says Deepthi. This collaborative approach ensures that both parties benefit from the partnership, creating a win-win situation.

Innovative Use of Technology: GoSports Foundation has embraced technology as a frugal force multiplier by delivering world-class coaching without the costs of dependence on coaches everywhere. 'Tech has enabled our identified academies to become world-class training centres,' says Deepthi, citing their collaboration with the Infosys Foundation. Through remote coaching, performance analysis and injury management tools, athletes across India gain access to top-tier expertise without leaving their hometowns. It's a lean, scalable model that builds a high-performance ecosystem.

GoSports Foundation's innovations demonstrate how strategic thinking and creativity can overcome resource constraints in Indian sports. By implementing a scholarship model, building an ecosystem on a budget, leveraging partnerships and CSR funding, and utilizing technology for remote coaching, the foundation has created sustainable pathways for athlete development.

Deepthi's leadership in turn shows how passion combined with innovative strategies can drive meaningful change: 'It's about finding a solution quicker and giving it some structure.' Through these efforts, GoSports Foundation continues to unlock India's sporting potential, paving the way for future generations of athletes who aspire to excel on the global stage.

Paralympics: A 'Judo Move'

GoSports Foundation's early decision to focus on para-sports stemmed from a clear recognition: athletes with disabilities face far greater challenges and receive far less support. This focus can be seen as both a 'judo move' and a strategic manoeuvre that leverages existing strengths and opportunities to overcome challenges. 'We were the first organization to actually start working with athletes with disability right from when we started,' says Deepthi Bopaiah. This foresight helped GoSports carve a niche in a space that had long been overlooked.

Para-sports also offer unique possibilities. With multiple classifications, more athletes get a shot at podium finishes. 'In badminton, for instance, you'll have about six or seven categories. And every category will have medals,' Deepthi explains. This structure makes para-sports inclusive and rewarding, both socially and strategically.

But achieving credibility in this space was key. By consistently supporting para-athletes and showing results, GoSports attracted CSR funding aligned with inclusion and impact. 'We had to make it about creating Olympians, Paralympians and rural sports development,' says Deepthi. The foundation's pitch, 'sport as a tool for inclusion', resonated with companies seeking meaningful CSR outcomes.

The foundation's reputation has only grown with time. 'We've never lost a donor in the last eight years,' Deepthi says, pointing to the strength of their systems and long-term relationships.

Indeed, GoSports-backed para-athletes have rewritten India's sporting script. From four medals at Rio 2016 to nineteen at Tokyo 2020, and twenty-nine at Paris 2024, India's rise has been remarkable. Gold medallists like Sumit Antil (javelin) and Avani Lekhara (rifle shooting) have become national icons.

Behind the medals is a frugal, intentional model: identify potential early, build lean support systems and amplify impact with technology and partnerships. GoSports didn't wait for perfect conditions—it created high-performance pathways using what was available.

Strengthen the Sports Ecosystem in India

'Jugaad isn't just coming up with solutions but being creative and open to failure,' says Deepthi. By embedding cost-effectiveness into its model, GoSports has shown how to stretch limited means into powerful results.

Mapping the Sports Landscape: India's sports landscape is complex and fragmented, with multiple stakeholders operating in silos. 'The system itself is so broken,' Deepthi notes, 'that our main focus is on keeping the ladder together and consistent.' Coordination gaps, especially in talent development, persist.

Programmes like Khelo India are steps forward, but gaps remain in nurturing talent from the grassroots to elite levels. As Deepthi says, 'Everyone is funding the top 200 athletes; we should focus on the next 2000.'

The Role of States and Federations: With sport being a state subject, state governments play a vital role in infrastructure and policy. However, their engagement is uneven. 'States need to actually start investing; there is no innovation happening at the state level,' Deepthi explains. Odisha stands out as a success story: combining political vision and strategic investment to turn hockey into a platform for broader state development. It shows how systemic innovation, done right, can ripple far beyond sport.

India's Potential in Sports Innovation: India's digital ecosystem and youthful talent base present a unique opportunity to lead in sports innovation. GoSports is already demonstrating how frugal solutions, like remote coaching and expert-driven, tech-enabled programmes can deliver high performance at low cost. 'We have experts from across the world trying to utilize that money in the best possible way,' says Deepthi.

A Pawn and a Punch: The Story of Two Deliberate Amateurs

How can sportspersons adopt the idea of frugality to become world class in their sport and compete on a global platform? The answer may lie in creating a generation of 'deliberate amateurs' across sports and disciplines.

The term 'amateur' derives from the Latin word *amator*, meaning 'lover'. It suggests an attitude of doing something for the love of it, not for the spotlight or the money. This mindset values learning through trial and error, staying curious, taking risks and keeping joy alive in the grind of training. It's not about being unprofessional; it's about being purposefully experimental—exactly the spirit that defines the LeanSpark approach.

The word 'deliberate' too has two meanings: to do something consciously and intentionally, and to do it in a careful, unhurried manner. When athletes combine this kind of intentionality with resourcefulness, using constraints as fuel rather than friction, they build something rare: a growth path that is sustainable, self-directed and scalable.

In a world chasing precision and perfection, the deliberate amateur quietly builds mastery. Whether it's a lone boxer training with borrowed gloves or a young chess player studying moves on a recycled board, the spark lies not in what they have, but in how they make it count.

Gukesh Dommaraju's meteoric rise in the chess world is a testament to the power of the deliberate amateur mindset of approaching challenges with curiosity, openness and a relentless drive to learn. Born in 2006 in Chennai, Gukesh began playing chess at the age of seven. His journey from novice to youngest World Chess Champion exemplifies how embracing an amateur's enthusiasm can lead to extraordinary achievements.

As a child, Gukesh spent countless hours studying the game and playing against opponents at all levels. Without access to top-tier coaching or facilities, he utilized available resources, including online platforms and local chess clubs, to hone his skills. This self-driven approach allowed him to develop a unique style and deep understanding of the game.

At twelve years and seven months, Gukesh became the second-youngest Grandmaster in history. His ascent didn't stop there; he continued to challenge himself against stronger opponents, participating in international tournaments to gain experience. In December 2024, he defeated reigning champion Ding Liren to become the youngest World Chess Champion at the age of eighteen, surpassing Garry Kasparov's record.

Despite reaching the pinnacle of chess, Gukesh remains grounded and continues to credit his success to a love for learning and an openness to new ideas, embodying the essence of the deliberate amateur mindset. By embracing this approach, he has not only achieved personal milestones but has also inspired a new generation of chess enthusiasts worldwide.

For sportspersons, frugality and being a deliberate amateur share a foundational ethos: doing more with less while embracing the joy of discovery and growth. Together, they inspire a way of thinking that is adaptable, innovative and focused on continuous learning.

Mary Kom's rise to the pinnacle of boxing is also a story of passion, perseverance and an unrelenting drive to improve her craft. Hailing from a modest farming family in Manipur, India, she had little exposure to professional boxing facilities or training early in her career. Her journey reflects the deliberate amateur mindset, where she embraced learning, experimentation and constant adaptation to refine her skills.

Mary was inspired to take up boxing after witnessing the success of Dingko Singh, another boxer from Manipur. Despite having no formal background in the sport, she approached it with enthusiasm, driven purely by her passion to explore something new. She started her training with minimal equipment, focusing on foundational skills like footwork, balance and stamina. She often learned by observing others, piecing together her technique through trial and error.

Mary relied on her improvisational skills to practice. She would use sandbags as punching bags and crafted her own fitness routines to build endurance and strength. She constantly experimented with combinations, defensive manoeuvres and her approach to footwork, treating each session as a chance to discover something new about herself and her sport.

Her deliberate amateur mindset meant she wasn't afraid to make mistakes. She viewed every sparring match, every punch and every movement as an opportunity to learn. Even after early success, she continued to refine her technique by exploring new strategies to outsmart opponents who were taller or stronger than her.

After becoming a mother, many doubted her ability to return to professional boxing. However, Mary approached this challenge with the same amateur mindset. She redesigned her training routine, balancing family responsibilities and practice. Mary's commitment to her craft culminated in her historic performances at the World Championships. She became the only woman to win the World Amateur Boxing Championship six times.

Gukesh's and Mary's journeys remind us that greatness often begins with a mindset of curiosity and exploration. By approaching their skills with the humility of a learner and the resilience of a champion, they rewrote what is possible in their respective fields. Their success is not just a testament to Indian sporting talent, it also proves that the deliberate amateur spirit can lead to extraordinary achievements.

Creating the Hall of Fame

Deepthi Bopaiah's journey from the predictability of banking to the unpredictable world of sport wasn't just a career pivot; it was a mindset shift. By asking better questions and designing lean systems that put athletes at the centre, she helped rewrite what success can look like in Indian sport.

This is LeanSpark in motion: moving fast but with thought, and building bold structures on humble foundations. Whether it's para-athletes rising to global podiums, young talent applying for scholarships instead of waiting to be spotted, or coaches using tech to train across distances, each spark is proof that impact doesn't always need opulence; it needs intention.

As Deepthi says, 'It's about finding solutions early and giving them structure.' This is true not just for sports in India, but for any nation that dares to dream big for its people.

3.2

Intelligence, Engineered
India's Frugal AI Revolution

On quiet evenings in the corridors of Jwalamukhi hostel at IIT Delhi, a young Vivek Raghavan would be debating; not just algorithms, but politics, development and the quirks of campus life. The son of a professor, raised in the academic environment of India's premier tech institute, Vivek had every reason to play it safe and live with his parents on the faculty side of campus. Instead he chose to live in the hostel, to immerse himself in the chaos and curiosity that defined student life.

Years later, after a PhD from Carnegie Mellon and two successful stints as a Silicon Valley entrepreneur, Vivek made another unorthodox choice: he returned home to India.

'I realized the real impact of technology could be felt more profoundly here,' he says. And with that belief, he turned his attention from designing chips to reimagining how identity, infrastructure and artificial intelligence could serve billions.

From Magma Design to Aadhaar to Beckn and beyond, Raghavan's career has followed a consistent arc of technology that scales, simplifies and is inclusive.

After returning to India in the late 2000s, Vivek joined the core technical team at the Unique Identification Authority of India (UIDAI). In Bangalore, he became part of a passionate group of volunteers, many from Google, Microsoft and Silicon Valley start-ups, brought together by Nandan Nilekani to work on Aadhaar. Vivek was soon appointed chief product manager and biometric architect, playing a central role in designing and implementing the system. For him and the team, Aadhaar wasn't just a technical challenge, it was a chance to use technology to create inclusive, citizen-centric solutions that could transform how the state delivered services.

Vivek later became chief mentor at AI4Bharat, an initiative developing AI tools in Indian languages. His work helped make technology more accessible across linguistic and regional divides, part of his larger mission to democratize tech for public good.

In this chapter, we explore how India and innovators like Vivek are shaping an approach to AI that is not just data-driven, but resource-aware and grounded in real-world needs. As we will see, unlike the lavishly funded, high compute and massive data models of the West, India's emerging AI stack is lean, affordable and inclusive.

AI4Bharat: Creating a Sovereign AI

In a world where AI development is dominated by a few global powers, sovereign AI, that is, artificial intelligence developed and owned by a country, is a necessity for self-reliance. For India, with its linguistic and economic diversity, building home-grown AI solutions is of critical strategic importance.

AI4Bharat, an initiative launched at IIT Madras in 2020, exemplifies this approach. It focuses on AI tools tailored for Indian languages and real-world constraints. Unlike Silicon Valley's compute-heavy models, AI4Bharat builds lightweight systems that run on low-end smartphones and low bandwidth networks, enabling access across the digital divide.

This is LeanSpark in action: solving large-scale problems under constraints of cost, bandwidth and infrastructure.

India is a mosaic of over 1600 dialects and twenty-two official languages. In such a multilingual society, the global models of AI built for English simply don't work. This is why sovereign AI, developed in India, is not a luxury but a necessity. It ensures that technology speaks the language of all people and not just the language of the rich. India's path forward in AI must be inclusive and open.

Founding Sarvam AI

'When ChatGPT came out in November 2023,' Vivek says, 'it simply blew my mind. Here was a truly deflationary technology in every sense of the term. Immediately I could see a way for India to achieve huge breakthroughs in health and education. Here was an opportunity to put a personal tutor in the pocket of every Indian child, and a personal physician in the hands of every Indian adult. An AI tutor, for instance, would cost far less than today's schools and provide much more personalized instruction.'

Generative AI, Vivek realized, could change lives in ways he hadn't imagined before or even thought possible. But it was crucial to build something that was suited to the Indian context: something that was highly affordable, scaled, based on voice and in Indian languages.

That was when Sarvam AI took shape. The company's mission would be to create scalable, cost-effective AI models that addressed the unique needs of Indian society. The start-up would develop full-stack AI solutions tailored to India's diverse linguistic and cultural landscape.

In all this, the vision for the company was deeply influenced by Vivek's belief in 'sovereign AI' models that respect data privacy and cultural nuances. The company would build on the frugal design principles that had influenced Aadhaar and UPI. The approach would involve open-sourcing AI models and collaborating with Indian enterprises to build domain-specific solutions. This strategy would not only foster innovation but also empower local researchers and developers to push the boundaries of AI technology.

Pratyush Kumar co-founded Sarvam AI with Vivek, after the two had worked together on AI4Bharat at IIT Madras. With a PhD from ETH Zurich and degrees from IIT Bombay, Pratyush brought deep expertise in AI and systems engineering to the partnership. He had previously worked at Microsoft Research, IBM Research and taught at IIT Madras. His work on AI4Bharat and PadhAI—an initiative to teach deep learning at scale—had helped spark his passion for making AI widely accessible and available.

Scaling Applications of Sarvam AI

When Pratyush and Vivek started Sarvam AI, they chose a for-profit model for the start-up, believing that to truly scale AI's impact across India, especially in areas like healthcare and education, significant investment and market competition were needed. As Vivek says: 'You can either sit on the sidelines or jump in yourself.' Sarvam AI's goal is to bring generative AI to 800 million Indians with smartphones, helping them use AI tools to improve their lives in meaningful ways.

In healthcare, Sarvam AI is deploying voice-enabled, multilingual conversational agents that allow rural patients to access medical advice, schedule appointments and consult doctors through WhatsApp and low-bandwidth interfaces. Their models, such as Sarvam 2B and Sarvam-M, are fine-tuned for medical reasoning and symptom triage in local languages, enabling tools that assist ASHA (Accredited Social Health Activist) workers and frontline clinics without the need for high-end devices or constant internet. These systems can summarize patient notes, offer diagnostic guidance and even prioritize cases, functioning as low-cost, frugal AI assistants for overstretched healthcare workers.

In the education sector, Sarvam AI is building sovereign, frugal solutions that cater to India's vast linguistic diversity. With its flagship model SarvamM, a 24-billion parameter large language model (LLM) trained across ten Indian languages, Sarvam enables vernacular learning assistants capable of understanding codemixed queries and delivering personalized instruction in students' mother tongues. These lightweight, optimized models empower AI tutors to adapt lessons in mathematics and programming to regional educational contexts, far beyond what English-centric platforms do. Early adopters include a Tamil Nadu NGO that deployed SarvamM in tribal schools via voice-based learning tools, resulting in a 40 per cent improvement in reading fluency within six months. Although uptake has been gradual, education experts emphasize that the model's multilingual logic puts India on the path towards truly inclusive AI tutoring, even in resource-constrained classrooms.

OpenHathi and Language Models

OpenHathi, developed by Sarvam AI, is a frugal and open-source project designed to teach Indian language skills to existing LLMs. Instead of building a model from scratch—an expensive and resource-heavy process—Sarvam adapted pre-trained models like Meta's LlaMA (short for Large Language Model Meta AI) and France's Mistral to understand Indian languages, starting with Hindi.

This was done in two steps: first, aligning Indian language meanings with the model's existing knowledge and then training it using bilingual texts so it could understand and generate content across languages. The result is a model that can handle translation, summarization and Q&A in Indian languages quickly, using far less energy.

As Vivek puts it, 'The idea is to bolt Indian language skills onto existing models. Once that's done, we can create smaller, domain-specific models in fields like finance or medicine that are much cheaper and more efficient to use.'

By building on open-source platforms and releasing models on Hugging Face, OpenHathi empowers developers to create local AI solutions in Indian languages—bringing sovereign AI closer to the people, one language at a time.

As Sarvam AI built its Indian language models, it ran into an unexpected challenge: Language costs money, quite literally! Not because of translation fees or licensing, but because of how AI breaks language down into tokens. A simple sentence in Hindi, for instance, required three to four times more tokens than the same sentence in English. That meant every AI interaction in an Indian language was significantly more expensive.

As Vivek puts it, 'The same question, when asked in English, costs one-fifth of what it costs in an Indian language.'

To address this, the Sarvam team didn't just complain, they innovated. They created better tokens for Indian languages and focused on building high-quality datasets to improve model performance without blowing up costs.

By tackling this problem at its root, Sarvam AI made it cheaper and more efficient to run AI models in Indian languages; an unsung but critical step towards making AI accessible for healthcare workers, students and everyday users across India.

Other Indian AI Start-Ups: Krutrim's Journey

Sarvam AI has Indian partners and competitors. In April 2023, Bhavish Aggarwal, the co-founder of Ola Cabs, launched Krutrim, an AI start-up focused on developing LLMs tailored for the Indian market. Together, Krutrim and Sarvam AI represent a growing trend in the Indian tech ecosystem, where home-grown start-ups are leveraging AI to address the country's specific needs and challenges.

Trained on over 2 trillion tokens, Krutrim can understand and generate text in twenty-two Indian languages, making it one of the most inclusive models designed for India's diverse population. But Krutrim's real power lies in its frugal DNA. Built with India's infrastructure in mind, it is optimized to run efficiently without the need for supercomputers. This makes it ideal for schools, start-ups and government services that want powerful AI at low cost.

While Sarvam AI focuses on Hindi and voice-first interfaces, Krutrim takes a broader approach with text generation across languages. Krutrim Pro, its advanced version, is designed to tackle complex tasks in Indic languages—an Indian challenger to GPT-4.

Their philosophies may differ—Krutrim aims to scale infrastructure, while Sarvam emphasizes localized, lightweight models—but both share a common mission: building sovereign AI for India, designed to serve the people, not just the privileged.

Together, Krutrim, Sarvam and a rising wave of Indian AI start-ups are rewriting the global AI playbook with solutions that are not only smart, but also scalable, affordable and multilingual. And they are not alone. India's burgeoning AI start-up ecosystem is home to several innovative ventures that are making significant strides in the field of generative AI. Three other notable start-ups that are driving this revolution include Beatoven.ai, Orbo AI and Qure.ai.

Beatoven.ai stands out for its unique application of AI to music generation. Founded in 2021 by Mansoor Rahimat Khan and Siddharth Bhardwaj, the start-up leverages advanced AI music generation techniques to produce high-quality, customizable tracks tailored to specific moods, genres and themes. This royalty-free background music can then be used for various creative projects. The start-up's approach is therefore centred around making high-quality music accessible and affordable. This is particularly relevant in the Indian context where content creators often face challenges in sourcing affordable and legally compliant music. By using AI to generate music, Beatoven.ai reduces the costs associated with traditional music licensing, making it an essential tool for video producers, podcasters and game developers. The platform's user-friendly interface allows users to customize music tracks based on parameters such as tempo, genre and emotion, ensuring that the output is tailored to their specific needs.

Orbo AI, based in Mumbai, is revolutionizing the beauty and personal care industry with its virtual make-up and hair-styling products. Founded by Manoj Shinde, Abhit Sinha and Danish Jamil in 2019, Orbo AI's technology allows users to try out products virtually, significantly increasing conversion rates for beauty brands. Their latest product, Beauty GPT, has further boosted their market presence by integrating generative AI capabilities to enhance user experience. Orbo AI's innovative approach not only transforms how consumers interact with beauty products but also provides valuable insights into brands, helping them optimize their product offerings and marketing strategies.

Qure.ai, founded by Prashant Warier and Pooja Rao in 2016, is a Mumbai-based start-up that uses AI to interpret medical imaging such as X-rays and CT scans. Qure.ai's technology provides quick and accurate diagnoses, which is crucial in India where there is a severe shortage of radiologists. By leveraging AI and machine learning algorithms, Qure.ai has helped over 1.6 crore patients worldwide, making it a significant player in the healthcare sector. Their AI-powered solutions are designed to assist healthcare professionals in diagnosing diseases more efficiently, thereby improving patient outcomes and reducing the burden on the healthcare system.

These start-ups reflect the growing power of India's AI ecosystem—solving local challenges with global relevance. Their success will depend on building AI that is not just cutting-edge, but also affordable, inclusive and context-aware. As Vivek Raghavan puts it, 'AI is so important that we need everyone working on it.'

Indeed, Vivek believes India has a unique opportunity to shape the future of AI, not by chasing massive, expensive models like those in Silicon Valley, but by focusing on frugal, purpose-driven AI that solves real problems. For India, the goal isn't Artificial General Intelligence (AGI). It's creating smaller, smarter models that are affordable, efficient and tailored for sectors like healthcare, education and agriculture.

One key shift he highlights is towards voice-based interfaces, which is a natural fit for India, where many people are more comfortable speaking than typing. AI-powered voice tools can help bridge the digital divide, especially for those in rural or low-literacy environments.

This India-first approach to AI—frugal, inclusive and multilingual—offers a blueprint for the Global South. As Vinod Khosla, the co-founder of Sun Microsystems and founder of Khosla Ventures, puts it, 'You can upgrade the skills of India's youth very quickly. We had a company that taught an Uber driver to do a cardiac ultrasound in a week—it was

FDA approved. That's the power of AI tutors. The countries that do this well will be the most competitive.'

Lessons for India from DeepSeek's Success

The rise of DeepSeek in China offers further insights for India's AI strategy, particularly in talent development, innovation culture and strategic autonomy. While India has a booming AI ecosystem with initiatives like AI4Bharat and Krutrim, there are still challenges in building a globally competitive AI industry.

Research and Talent Development: In terms of talent, China has significantly increased the number of its STEM and AI graduates while reducing the brain drain to the West. India, too, has world-class institutions like the IITs, IIITs and IISc, but it needs to invest more in research to build a deep tech ecosystem. India can scale AI research at lower costs by investing in affordable AI training programs through open-source AI models like AI4Bharat. Strengthening public–private partnerships for AI fellowships can provide top researchers with funding and industry exposure without requiring them to leave India. China's AI growth benefits from strong ties between universities and enterprises, allowing research to transition to market-ready products.

AI Infrastructure: China is developing its own AI cloud and semiconductor supply chain to reduce reliance on Western AI platforms. Low-cost AI hardware innovation, such as energy-efficient AI chips developed through collaborations with IITs and indigenous semiconductor firms will be critical for the AI ecosystem to thrive in India. The launch of India's first fully designed AI server by VVDN Technologies in Kochi in April 2025 is a significant development. The eight-GPU AI server is part of the next generation supercomputer Param and a major contributor to the national mission on artificial intelligence.

Regulatory Flexibility: DeepSeek succeeded partly because it stayed under the radar of China's regulatory crackdowns. In contrast, India has a growing but complex regulatory landscape for AI which, if not handled carefully, could stifle innovation. The Indian entrepreneurship ecosystem needs to provide sandboxes for AI start-ups, allowing them to experiment with minimal compliance costs. The government needs to focus on policy support for AI in frugal sectors like agriculture (precision farming AI), healthcare (affordable diagnostics) and finance (AI-driven financial inclusion).

That said, India's AI journey need not follow China's state-heavy model. Instead, it should chart its own path by building on its strengths of scalable digital infrastructure and open-source ecosystems. Initiatives like AI4Bharat and Krutrim reflect this vision: creating inclusive, indigenous AI tailored for India's linguistic and socio-economic complexity. However, while these efforts signal promise, they are not without obstacles. From data scarcity and compute limitations to language diversity and funding gaps, both AI4Bharat and Krutrim face significant challenges in translating their vision into sustainable, large-scale impact. Understanding these barriers is key to strengthening India's sovereign AI future.

Challenges for AI4Bharat and Krutrim

While AI4Bharat has made impressive strides with open-source models like IndicBERT and IndicTrans, it continues to grapple with India's severe data scarcity. With over 1500 dialects, high-quality, diverse datasets for all Indian languages simply don't exist, forcing the team to build benchmarks and collect parallel corpora from scratch, which is a labour-intensive and time-consuming task. Meanwhile, Krutrim, trained on 2 trillion tokens across twenty-two languages, faces a different set of hurdles. Its success depends on domestic AI infrastructure: Indian firms need access to efficient, cost-effective hardware such as GPUs and chips. As Krutrim's executive A. Navendu points out, without these, scaling foundational model training remains difficult.

Many industry veterans have acknowledged these challenges and have a view on how India can address them. Vivek Raghavan, drawing from his experience with Aadhaar and UPI, emphasizes the power of building incrementally—what he calls 'plus-one thinking'. Just as UPI layered on top of IMPS to create a universal, low-cost digital payment system, AI solutions too can scale by building on existing infrastructure and open-source models. He notes how simple interventions, like standardized QR codes and zero-cost transactions, unlocked digital access even for street vendors.

Others echo this approach. Mohandas Pai argues that India should focus on domain-specific AI like healthcare and agriculture, rather than chasing massive foundation models. Nandan Nilekani adds that India's digital stack uniquely positions it to adopt AI quickly and inclusively, especially in local languages and through voice-based interfaces.

By combining layered innovation, regional AI hubs beyond metros and public–private fellowship programmes to retain top researchers, India has the opportunity to build an affordable, sovereign AI ecosystem designed for population-scale impact.

Lessons from India's AI Playbook

What if the world didn't need billion-dollar labs to build powerful AI? What if the future of artificial intelligence could be shaped in dusty classrooms, crowded clinics and village panchayats?

India is showing how this might be possible. From voice-based tutors in tribal schools to open-source AI trained on Indian languages, India's frugal approach to innovation offers a bold new playbook, especially for countries facing similar constraints. Instead of copying Silicon Valley, India is building its own path: low-cost, locally rooted and globally relevant. In other words, India has adopted the LeanSpark approach. Other countries can benefit by following suit.

Focus on Local Needs: Rather than simply importing AI solutions developed in the West, India has focused on creating AI models and applications that are tailored to its specific challenges and opportunities. This approach ensures that AI is not just a technological novelty but a tool for driving real-world impact and social change.

Create an Open, Collaborative Ecosystem: India has actively encouraged partnerships between government, industry and academia to foster the development of AI technologies.

Initiatives like AI4Bharat and Sarvam AI demonstrate the power of collaborative efforts in advancing AI research and innovation. By pooling resources, expertise and data, these partnerships can accelerate the pace of AI development and ensure that the benefits of AI are widely distributed.

Focus on the Common Good: India's emphasis on responsible AI is also a valuable lesson for the world. As AI becomes increasingly pervasive, it is crucial to ensure that its development and deployment are guided by ethical principles and a commitment to social good. By prioritizing the development of responsible AI frameworks and guidelines, India is setting a positive example for other countries to follow.

Develop an AI Workforce: Furthermore, India's approach to AI education and skill development offers insights into how countries can prepare their workforce for the AI-driven future. By incorporating AI education into school curricula and promoting digital literacy, India is laying the foundation for a tech-savvy generation that can harness the power of AI for innovation and entrepreneurship. This focus on AI education is not limited to technical skills but also includes an emphasis on developing critical thinking, creativity and problem-solving abilities, which are essential for thriving in an AI-driven world.

Be Mindful of Sovereignty: A crucial aspect of India's AI strategy is its focus on technology and data sovereignty. As highlighted by Vivek and other experts, India recognizes the importance of owning and controlling its data and developing AI solutions that respect privacy and adhere to local laws. This approach ensures that India's AI development is aligned with its national interests and values, rather than being dictated by external forces.

India's journey in AI shows that innovation doesn't need to be expensive to be impactful. By combining frugality with purpose, and technology with inclusion, India is crafting a model that works not just for itself, but for the world. As sovereign AI ecosystems like AI4Bharat, Sarvam AI and Krutrim grow, they offer powerful lessons in how to build ethical, local and scalable solutions under constraints.

The age of Frugal AI has only just begun.

3.3

Lean Bytes, Big Ideas
Transforming Governance for a Billion

In July 2009, Nandan Nilekani, co-founder and former CEO of India's outsourcing giant Infosys, received an unusual call. It was from Prime Minister Dr Manmohan Singh. The PM had invited Nandan to join the Government of India as chairman of the Unique Identification Authority of India (UIDAI). His task would be as bold as it was simple: to revolutionize governance in India using the tools and approaches he had pioneered in the private sector.

This was not an easy decision. Nandan had recently stepped down from Infosys, where he had built a formidable legacy as a pioneer of the Indian IT industry. Public administration was uncharted territory, and the challenges ahead were daunting. And yet, the prospect of giving back to the nation and creating a system that could transform millions of lives inspired him to accept the role.

At the heart of the mission was Aadhaar, a unique identification number for every Indian linked to their biometric and demographic data. The need for such a system was pressing. In a country where half the population lacked any formal identification, millions of Indians were effectively invisible to the state. This barred them from accessing essential services and benefits, leaving them vulnerable to exploitation by middlemen who used their identities to siphon off resources meant for the needy.

'The problem at that time was that over 500 million Indians had no means of proving who they were,' Nandan explains. 'We had to solve this problem to ensure that those for whom government benefits were intended actually received them.'

Aadhaar became a landmark in innovation by using existing technology and infrastructure to build a scalable, efficient ID system across India. Despite its complexity, it was rolled out quickly and cost effectively, reaching 500 million people in five years, and the entire country by 2018. What was achieved at a cost of $1 per ID in India compares to $34 in the US, $20 in the UAE and about $10 in Africa.

This streamlined access to government services would go on to save the state billions by eliminating fake beneficiaries. How did India achieve this scale and efficiency using relatively new technologies, while outpacing more developed countries in technical and social innovation?

Aadhaar: The Foundation

In the late 2000s, India was grappling with a fragmented system of identity verification. Citizens relied on a patchwork of documents, such as voter IDs, ration cards and passports, each serving different purposes and often leading to duplication and fraud. This absence of a standardized ID created barriers to accessing essential services, particularly for marginalized communities.

In his 2008 book *Imagining India: The Idea of a Renewed Nation*, Nandan recognized the challenge of identity that India faced. The solution he proposed was a single, universally recognized number linked to a citizen's unique biometrics. Such an ID would ensure that government benefits reached their intended recipients. As he explains, 'The country needed a unique and universal ID for every Indian. This would not only ensure that the citizens for whom government benefits are intended would receive them, in a fair and efficient way, but also eliminate fraud in the system and save the state huge sums.'

In May 2009, India had just completed holding its national elections. The incumbent Indian National Congress had been re-elected. This was when Prime Minister Dr Manmohan Singh approached Nandan about working with his team. 'After a couple of conversations,' Nandan says, 'I realized that working on a unique ID was the right thing for me to do. I could see its value. It was technology-intensive, which played to my strengths, and its potential success was clearly measurable.'

Nandan's appointment as UIDAI chairman in July 2009 marked a turning point for Aadhaar. He visualized it as a tool for inclusion—helping individuals access services and benefits seamlessly across India.

Aware of the political and bureaucratic challenges, he pushed for rapid rollout to minimize delays and interference.

His strategic engagement with central and state governments, and his ability to assemble a capable team of technocrats, helped overcome initial roadblocks and build acceptance for the project.

Launched in September 2010, Aadhaar aimed to provide a twelve-digit unique ID linked to biometric and demographic data. The first number was issued on 29 September 2010, in Nandurbar, Maharashtra. The project targeted identity fraud, increased transparency and improved delivery of public services.

Aadhaar's Development

Aadhaar's development was marked by several innovations that enabled its rapid and cost-effective implementation. These innovations were crucial in achieving the project's ambitious goals within budget constraints.

Minimal Data Collection: Only essential biometric (fingerprints, iris scans) and demographic data (name, age, gender, address) were collected. This reduced the technical complexity, cost of hardware and storage, and minimized privacy concerns, making the process faster and more scalable. As Nilekani said, 'I wanted to keep the solution simple.'

Open Standards for Biometric Devices: UIDAI only defined the technical standards for biometric hardware and software (instead of buying and maintaining the equipment). This allowed multiple vendors to supply compatible devices, which in turn encouraged competition and significantly drove down costs. It also sped up deployment by decentralizing procurement.

Decentralized, Demand-Led Enrolment: The project made enrolment free and voluntary, and clearly communicated its benefits to the citizens of India, such as access to services and subsidies. This created a bottom-up pull as people wanted Aadhaar, reducing the burden on the state to push adoption. The voluntary nature built public trust and increased participation.

Leveraged Existing Infrastructure: UIDAI partnered with banks, post offices and state governments who then acted as registrars to collect enrolment data. This avoided the creation of a new bureaucratic structure. By using existing trusted entities, the project saved money, tapped into local trust networks and accelerated rollout.

Cultivated a Partnership Ecosystem: The UIDAI team focused only on building the core software platform, while outsourcing other tasks (like device supply, enrolment and outreach) to partners. As Vivek Raghavan, the chief product manager and biometric architect, puts it, 'We knew we couldn't do many of these things on our own.' This modular structure and lean execution allowed for rapid scaling without overburdening the central team.'

These innovations together demonstrated how a frugal, partnership-driven approach could help solve complex public challenges without large capital outlays, and could do so by combining lean systems thinking with social inclusivity.

Impact on Governance: Streamlining Services

Aadhaar transformed governance in India by improving public service delivery and transparency. A key application was direct benefit transfers (DBT), linking subsidies directly to beneficiaries' Aadhaar-linked bank accounts. The PAHAL scheme, launched in 2014, used Aadhaar to transfer LPG subsidies, cutting out ghost beneficiaries. This led to a 24 per cent drop in subsidized gas sales and saved $2 billion in 2014–15: more than the project's total cost.

Aadhaar also enabled the JAM (Jan Dhan–Aadhaar–Mobile) trinity, integrating financial inclusion, digital ID and mobile access. Finance Minister Arun Jaitley called it crucial for reducing leakages and ensuring inclusion.

Other initiatives included DigiLocker (for digital document storage) and direct food subsidy transfers. By 2016, Aadhaar-linked food subsidies saved the country $4.8 billion annually.

Aadhaar was widely praised. Nobel Laureate Paul Romer called it 'the most sophisticated ID program in the world' and a potential global model.

Aadhaar stands as a milestone in digital identity, proving how frugal innovation and leadership can drive large-scale, inclusive reform. As Nandan says, 'If you build the right digital infrastructure, then you can leapfrog.'

Unified Payments Interface: Revolutionizing Payments in India

UPI, launched in April 2016, is a real-time payment system that enables users to link multiple bank accounts to a single mobile application, facilitating seamless peer-to-peer (P2P) and peer-to-merchant (P2M) transaction. UPI's primary goal was to simplify interbank transactions and promote the widespread adoption of digital payments across India. Nilekani has described UPI as a game-changer in India's digital payment landscape, revolutionizing the way people transact and paving the way for a cashless economy.

UPI's success can be attributed to several frugal innovations that made it a low-cost and scalable solution. By utilizing existing banking infrastructure and adopting a platform-centric approach, UPI minimizes the need for additional physical infrastructure, such as bank branches or ATMs, thereby reducing overhead costs.

UPI allows users to link multiple bank accounts to one mobile application. This significantly simplifies digital payments and makes them more accessible to a wider audience, especially for first-time users and those in rural areas. By building on Aadhaar's e-KYC system, UPI slashed identity verification costs from ₹500 to just ₹3. This drastically lowered onboarding costs for banks and fintechs, enabling rapid expansion of digital financial services to under-served populations.

UPI's open API model allowed any bank or fintech to integrate easily, fostering a level playing field. This design enabled platforms like Google Pay, PhonePe and Paytm to coexist, creating a vibrant, competitive ecosystem that benefited users through better service and lower costs. To build confidence in low-connectivity areas, UPI-enabled vendors used sound boxes that provided audible transaction confirmations. This small yet powerful device reassured both payers and payees that payments had gone through, demonstrating UPI's commitment to inclusive design.

Fostering a Fintech Ecosystem

UPI has also provided a major boost for India's fintech ecosystem, offering a platform for start-ups to innovate around and grow. The ease of integration and low transaction costs have enabled start-ups to attract a broad customer base, ranging from tech-savvy millennials to users in rural areas. This democratization of access to digital payment systems has been instrumental in the rise of numerous fintech unicorns.

As of mid-2025, India was home to thirty fintech unicorns, with consumer financing emerging as a dominant segment. Start-ups like Paytm and PhonePe have successfully leveraged UPI to expand their user base, initially focusing on UPI-based transactions before diversifying into a range of financial services, from wealth management to lending. The fintech sector in India has raised significant capital, with reports indicating a total of $5.7 billion in funding, reflecting the sector's potential. Observing UPI's influence, Nandan Nilekani says, 'The advent of UPI has been particularly significant for fintech start-ups in India, offering them a powerful tool to innovate, attract customers and expand their service portfolios.'

Globally, India ranks third in the number of fintech unicorns, after the United States and China. This rapid growth underscores the country's emergence as a major player in the global fintech landscape, driven by the widespread adoption of UPI and the supportive regulatory environment fostered by the National Payments Corporation of India and the Indian government.

Open Networks: Democratizing Access

The Open Network for Digital Commerce (ONDC) is transforming India's e-commerce landscape by shifting from platform-based models to an open, decentralized network. Inspired by internet-era open protocols, ONDC aims to break the monopolies of traditional platforms and create a more inclusive and competitive digital economy.

The journey began with the Beckn Protocol in 2018, designed to enable peer-to-peer digital transactions across sectors. Beckn laid the foundation for ONDC by promoting interoperability and decentralization. ONDC had secured funding of $32 million and launched pilot programmes in five cities by April 2022.

In January 2023, ONDC handled 2000 monthly transactions. By April 2024, this had grown to 7.5 million monthly transactions, involving 7.5 million sellers, 4,50,000 SKUs and operations in eighty-five cities. This scale-up shows the potential of open networks to empower small businesses and reduce entry barriers.

ONDC's success stems from its LeanSpark-inspired design. By building on existing systems like UPI, using open APIs and removing intermediaries, it keeps costs low and integration easy. Its decentralized structure ensures there is no single gatekeeper, opening up fair access for small businesses and sparking innovation across the board.

As Sujith Nair, co-creator of Beckn, puts it: 'Open networks enable equitable access and opportunities.' That is the promise ONDC is beginning to deliver on: namely, creating a more inclusive, affordable and open digital commerce ecosystem.

And as Pramod Varma, co-architect of Aadhaar, India Stack and Beckn Protocol, adds, 'If you make the rails open and inter-operable, and population scale from day one, innovation at the edges becomes both inevitable and affordable.'

Open networks are now expanding beyond e-commerce into sectors like mobility and energy. Namma Yatri, launched in Bangalore in November 2022, is a peer-to-peer mobility platform that connects drivers directly to passengers. It removes intermediaries, making rides cheaper for users and more profitable for drivers. By June 2024, it had over 3,69,000 drivers, 6.7 million users and was facilitating 1,15,000 rides daily, generating $61 million in driver earnings.

Similarly, the Unified Energy Interface (UEI), launched in February 2024, is creating an open network for energy services such as EV charging, battery use and peer-to-peer energy-sharing. In its first three months, UEI handled over 2,20,000 transactions, covering 1560 MWh of energy.

Together, initiatives like ONDC, Namma Yatri and UEI show how open, decentralized networks can reduce costs, improve access and drive innovation, creating a more inclusive and sustainable digital economy.

When Frugality Fumbles: Challenges of Digital Transformation

While Aadhaar, UPI and ONDC represent remarkable successes in frugal innovation, the approach also has challenges that warrant attention.

Security and Privacy Concerns: Frugal innovation, while driving cost efficiency, can come at the expense of robust security and data protection. Aadhaar has faced significant criticism for potential vulnerabilities in its centralized database. Privacy advocates warn that the focus on rapid deployment and scalability can compromise the robustness of data protection mechanisms, leaving sensitive biometric data exposed to risks of breaches and misuse.

As digital platforms like Aadhaar and UPI expand, they become increasingly attractive targets for cyberattacks. Scaling these systems securely requires substantial investment in advanced cybersecurity tools, skilled personnel and rigorous processes—investments that are often at odds with the principles of frugal innovation. Without prioritizing security as a non-negotiable cornerstone, the vulnerabilities inherent in these systems risk undermining public trust.

Burgeoning Digital Divide: The reliance on digital platforms assumes a baseline level of digital literacy and access to technology, which is not universal in India. UPI and ONDC depend on smartphones and internet connectivity, leaving out a significant portion of rural or economically disadvantaged populations. This can exacerbate existing inequalities, limiting the benefits for those who need these services the most. The intention of inclusion could potentially lead to further exclusion of the same citizens.

Over-reliance on Ecosystem Participants: Frugal systems often delegate significant responsibilities to third-party participants, such as private companies or local agencies. Aadhaar's enrolment process involved private agencies, some of which might have engaged in questionable practices, undermining the platform's credibility. UPI and ONDC rely on standardized APIs, but variations in implementation among banks, fintech firms and vendors can create inconsistencies and reduce user experience quality. These issues can lead to fragmentation, hampering the seamless experience the platforms aim to provide.

Lessons from India's Progress in Digital Public Infrastructure

Despite these limitations, India's digital public infrastructure (DPI) is a powerful testament to the transformative potential of technology in fostering inclusive growth and development. From Aadhaar's groundbreaking identity system to the revolutionary UPI, India's experience offers valuable lessons and best practices for implementing frugal innovation in public sector projects.

Plus-One Thinking: A key takeaway from India's digital journey is the power of building on what already exists. Instead of starting from scratch, India used its widespread mobile network and low-cost data to create a strong digital foundation. This approach, which Vivek Raghavan calls 'plus-one thinking', adds new layers of innovation onto existing systems to extend reach and capability.

Aadhaar was the starting point. Once in place, it enabled the creation of India Stack, a layered digital ecosystem. Features like digital signatures, lockers and wallets were built on top of Aadhaar, enabling secure data storage and transactions. These, in turn, laid the groundwork for UPI and e-KYC, which used Aadhaar for identity verification to enable seamless, real-time payments. This strategy of incremental innovation has helped

India stretch its resources while rapidly scaling digital access and services.

Becoming Data-Rich (While Still Economically Poor): India recognized the immense value of data early on and took proactive steps to create data-rich environments to drive public governance. Initiatives like Aadhaar, UPI and the ONDC framework have enabled the collection and utilization of vast amounts of data, empowering citizens and driving economic growth. As Amitabh Kant, CEO of NITI Aayog, emphasizes, 'Data is the new oil, and India is sitting on a gold mine of data.'

Planning for Scale and Designing for Affordability: India's digital initiatives were conceived with the goal of reaching every citizen, regardless of their socio-economic status or geographic location. By prioritizing simplicity, affordability and ease of use, projects like Aadhaar and UPI have achieved massive scale and adoption.

Indeed, designing for scale and affordability has been a cornerstone of India's approach, ensuring that digital solutions are accessible to all segments of the population. This focus on LeanSpark thinking has been instrumental in driving widespread adoption and impact, demonstrating that scale provides affordability. As Vivek explains the conundrum, 'To be affordable, you have to scale. And to scale, you must be affordable.'

A Digital Playbook for the World

India's story shows what's possible when technology, public purpose and smart design come together. The country's digital public infrastructure, from Aadhaar to UPI, has become a powerful example of how innovation can be inclusive, affordable and scalable. It's not just about tools or platforms, but about reimagining how governments serve people. This is the heart of the LeanSpark mindset: building solutions that work for millions (and billions) without losing sight of those at the margins.

India's model stands apart because it combines openness, interoperability and competition while keeping citizen rights at the centre. As Nandan puts it, 'India Stack is a template for the world'—a reminder that a developing country can build world-class digital systems that empower its citizens.

As more countries look to adopt similar ideas, the world has a real opportunity to shape a shared digital future. If done correctly India's approach could spark a global shift towards digital ecosystems that truly empower, include and uplift.

3.4

Indra Ascending

Indian Prowess in Space

23 August 2023, 18.04 GMT. The air in the control room at the Indian Space Research Organization's Satellite Control Centre in Bengaluru is thick with anticipation. The palpable tension crackles like electricity. The women and men of ISRO, in colourful saris and crisp white shirts, lean forward in their seats, eyes glued to screens flickering with data streams and telemetry readouts. They are the chosen few, the cream of India's scientific crop, entrusted with a task that will make or break the nation's dreams of lunar conquest.

Outside, the subcontinent holds its breath. From the bustling streets of Mumbai to the serene banks of the Ganga, a billion hearts beat in unison, all tuned to the cosmic dance unfolding 3,84,400 kilometres away. The Chandrayaan-3 lander, aptly named Vikram after Vikram Sarabhai, the father of India's space programme, is making its final descent onto the moon's treacherous south pole.

In the preceding days, the Russians have fumbled in their lunar ambitions, their Luna-25 craft now nothing more than a fresh impact crater on the moon's unforgiving surface. The south pole, with its jagged terrain and shadowy craters, has proven to be a siren's call, luring spacecraft to their doom. But here is India, the underdog, the nation of jugaad and frugal innovation, daring to tread where giants had stumbled. Will the country whose space ambitions exceed its ability to finance them succeed where many other far richer nations have failed? Will an approach which relies on frugality, adaptability and purposeful ingenuity succeed where others have failed?

As Vikram enters the final phase of its descent, a hush falls over the control room. The lander's thrusters fire in short, controlled bursts, each one a testament to years of meticulous planning and the kind of engineering that has squeezed miracles out of shoestring budgets. On the main screen, a 3D rendering of the lander inches closer to the lunar surface, its trajectory a gossamer thread of hope stretching across the void.

Suddenly, a voice crackles over the speakers: 'Touchdown confirmed!' The room erupts. Cheers, tears and embraces sweep through the ranks of scientists and engineers like a tsunami of joy. Men wearing glasses pump their fists; women in saris clasps their hands in prayer, eyes glistening with pride.

In this moment, India has done the impossible. A nation ranked 129th in the world in GDP per capita and 134th in human development has just planted its flag where only the wealthiest and most technologically advanced nations have dared to venture. It is a victory not just for India, but for the very spirit of human ingenuity.

As news of the landing spreads, streets across India burst into celebrations. Fireworks light up the night, their thunderous noise a twenty-one-gun salute to the quiet heroes in Bengaluru. In the control room, amidst the chaos of triumph, a senior scientist pauses, his weathered face etched with lines of determination and now, finally, relief. He turns to a younger colleague, eyes twinkling with a mix of exhaustion and exhilaration, and says, 'We did it. We really did.'

And so they had. With a stubborn resolve, with late nights and early mornings, with cups of chai and dreams as vast as the cosmos itself, the men and women of ISRO had written a new chapter in the annals of space exploration. India had arrived on the moon, and the world would never be the same again.

How on earth did India pull off such a feat? How, moreover, had it done so on such a tight budget: at a mere $70 million, a fraction of what NASA's similar missions had cost?

How ISRO Embraced the Idea of LeanSpark

The genesis of ISRO can be traced back to the early 1960s when Dr Vikram Sarabhai, often hailed as the father of India's space programme, recognized the potential of space technology to address the country's developmental needs.

From its inception, ISRO's mission was clear: to harness space technology for national development. This mission was a direct response to the many challenges India faced. In a country where millions of farmers depended on the monsoon rains for their livelihood, the potential of weather satellites to improve agricultural forecasting was immense. Similarly, in a vast and diverse nation with many remote areas, communication satellites offered the promise of bridging the information gap and fostering national integration.

ISRO's early years were characterized by frugal innovation borne out of necessity. With limited funds and restricted access to advanced technology due to international sanctions, Indian scientists and engineers had to rely on their native ingenuity and resourcefulness.

From Frugal to Deliberate Design

The concept of frugal innovation is deeply rooted in Indian culture, representing a unique design approach to problem-solving that has both shaped and been shaped by the country's socio-economic landscape.

This approach is characterized by its emphasis on flexibility and inclusivity. It often involves repurposing existing resources or finding unconventional uses for ubiquitous tools to solve pressing problems. This mindset has given rise to numerous innovations, from simple household hacks to more sophisticated technological solutions.

However, this approach has its limitations. While it fosters creativity and quick problem-solving, it can lead to haphazard, short-term fixes that lack scalability. When things are 'hacked' together, they often don't scale well, potentially compromising long-term effectiveness and quality.

Recognizing both the strengths and limitations of improvisational problem-solving, organizations like ISRO have steadily moved towards more structured and purposeful innovation. This marks a maturing of India's innovation landscape, where the spirit of creativity under constraint is now being blended with rigorous design thinking, long-term planning and a focus on scale.

Importantly, this shift doesn't mean discarding the original mindset of working smartly with what's available. Instead, it is about transforming that instinctive approach into a more thoughtful and strategic one. The aim is to build solutions that are not just clever and affordable but also reliable, repeatable and capable of creating widespread impact.

This evolution in thinking has been central to ISRO's journey over the years. It highlights an important lesson for India's broader innovation story, that while quick fixes and intuitive solutions have their place, they need to be backed by systems, strategy and deliberate design if they are to truly change the world.

Fuels Rockets and Satellites

The development of India's first satellite, Aryabhata, launched in 1975, showcased ISRO's frugal mindset. For instance, owing to limited funds and facilities, ISRO scientists converted a dilapidated building into a data receiving centre for the satellite. This unconventional approach allowed them to meet necessary standards without the expense of building a new facility from scratch.

ISRO's mindset has consistently reflected principles of frugal ingenuity. Instead of attempting to build advanced rockets from the outset, ISRO adopted a step-by-step approach, gradually improving its capabilities. The Satellite Launch

Vehicle (SLV) programme, which began in the 1970s, used this incremental strategy. Each version of the SLV built upon lessons learned from its predecessor, allowing ISRO to develop increasingly sophisticated rockets without the budgets of other space agencies.

The development of the Polar Satellite Launch Vehicle (PSLV), ISRO's workhorse rocket, is another example of frugal innovation. ISRO engineers designed the PSLV to be versatile and cost-effective, capable of launching satellites into various orbits. This flexibility eventually made the PSLV attractive to international customers, generating revenue for ISRO and offsetting development costs.

ISRO's Mars Orbiter Mission (MOM), also known as Mangalyaan, launched in 2013, is perhaps the most celebrated example of the LeanSpark approach in space exploration. Completed at a fraction of the cost of similar missions by other space agencies, Mangalyaan showcased ISRO's ability to achieve complex objectives with limited resources. The mission, which cost less than the $100 million budget of the Hollywood film *Gravity*, became a testament to the power of frugal innovation.

Indeed, the mission's success can be attributed to several innovative strategies.

Reusing and Repurposing Existing Technologies: ISRO adapted technologies from its lunar mission, Chandrayaan-1, for Mangalyaan, reducing development time and costs.

Innovative Orbit-Raising Manoeuvres: Instead of using a powerful rocket to send the spacecraft directly to Mars, ISRO used a series of orbit-raising manoeuvres around Earth to gradually build up the necessary velocity. This approach, while taking longer, significantly reduced fuel requirements and launch costs.

A Focus on Core Objectives: ISRO focused on essential scientific objectives, avoiding unnecessary complexities that would have increased costs.

Efficient Project Management: The project was completed in just eighteen months: a remarkably short time for an interplanetary mission. This was achieved by leveraging ISRO's existing expertise and parallel processing ability.

Overall, Mangalyaan's success demonstrated India's space capabilities while showcasing the potential of frugal ingenuity on a global stage. It proved that breakthrough achievements in space exploration could be possible without massive budgets. This challenged conventional wisdom in the aerospace industry.

ISRO's Chandrayaan missions to the moon further exemplify its frugal approach. Chandrayaan-2, despite its partial failure in the landing attempt, demonstrated several innovative solutions. The mission combined an orbiter, lander and rover in a single launch, maximizing the scientific output while minimizing launch costs. Although the lander crashed, the orbiter continues to function, providing valuable data and demonstrating the mission's overall cost-effectiveness.

The successful Chandrayaan-3 mission in 2023, which achieved a soft landing on the moon's south pole region, built upon the lessons learned from Chandrayaan-2. ISRO engineers refined the lander design, improved the landing algorithms, and conducted more rigorous testing—all while maintaining a budget far lower than comparable international missions. This success not only marked a significant achievement for India but also validated ISRO's LeanSpark-inspired approach to space exploration.

ISRO's mindset isn't only about finding makeshift solutions; it's also about fostering a culture of innovation and resourcefulness. The organization encourages its scientists and engineers to think creatively, challenge conventional approaches and find efficient solutions to complex problems. This culture has enabled ISRO to consistently punch above its weight in the global space arena.

It is important also to note that ISRO's application of LeanSpark principles does not imply that it compromises on quality or safety. The organization maintains rigorous standards and has developed sophisticated quality assurance processes. LeanSpark at ISRO is about smart resource allocation, innovative problem-solving and maximizing output from available inputs.

As ISRO looks to the future, with ambitious plans for human spaceflight, further lunar exploration and interplanetary missions, this mindset continues to evolve. The organization is increasingly focusing on reusable launch vehicles, in-situ resource utilization and other cutting-edge technologies. These efforts demonstrate how such thinking can align with, and drive, advanced technological development.

Scaling New Heights

ISRO's success with frugal innovation hasn't been limited to Earth-orbiting satellites or lunar missions. The organization has leveraged its expertise and cost-effective approaches to venture further into the solar system, with ambitious missions to Mars, the sun and plans for Venus. These projects demonstrate how ISRO continues to push the boundaries of space exploration while maintaining its commitment to frugal innovation.

Building on the success of Mangalyaan, on 2 September 2023, ISRO launched the Aditya-L1 mission, India's first space-based solar observatory. Aditya-L1 is designed to study the sun's outermost layer, the corona, along with solar emissions and their impact on space weather.

True to ISRO's frugal innovation approach, Aditya-L1 was developed at a fraction of the cost of similar missions by other space agencies. The mission utilized the proven PSLV rocket, further reducing costs. ISRO again optimized the payload, focusing on seven essential instruments that provide valuable data on solar phenomena.

One of the key innovations in Aditya-L1 is positioning at the L1 Lagrange point, approximately 1.5 million kilometres from Earth. This location offers an uninterrupted view of the sun and allows for continuous observation without eclipses. Achieving this complex orbital manoeuvre with limited resources showcases ISRO's ability to maximize scientific output while minimizing costs.

Despite all this progress, however, ISRO now stands at a crossroads. Global competition from the developed and emerging world is heating up. The challenges are many. How will the organization respond?

ISRO at a Crossroads

India's space programme has been celebrated for its ability to achieve ambitious missions on shoestring budgets. However, the global landscape in space has grown increasingly complex, with powerful new entrants challenging established players.

In the US, SpaceX has achieved breakthroughs with its reusable rockets, including using the same Falcon 9 booster more than fifteen times. This capability has enabled SpaceX to launch satellites at substantially lower costs while maintaining high reliability. The company's approach combines frugal principles with significant upfront investment in transformative technology.

Meanwhile, China has embarked on an aggressive expansion of its space capabilities, posing a serious challenge to ISRO's position. The country has announced plans for multiple mega-constellations, including Spacesail (Qianfan), a 15,000-satellite constellation aiming to rival Starlink, with 197 satellites already in orbit and plans for 600 by the end of 2025; Guowang, a planned 13,000-satellite network; and Honghu-3, a 10,000-satellite constellation. China aims to capture 8 per cent of the global space market by 2033, growing its space economy to $44 billion. While currently limited by its reliance on expendable rockets, Chinese firms are developing reusable launch systems like SpaceX's Falcon 9.

As global space competition intensifies with disruptive players like SpaceX and ambitious national programmes from China, ISRO faces challenges that demand a reimagining of its frugal innovation model.

The Limitations of Incremental Innovation: ISRO's historical approach to space exploration has centred around incremental innovation and meticulous cost engineering. The PSLV, ISRO's reliable workhorse, epitomizes this philosophy: a rocket developed through gradual improvements over decades rather than revolutionary leaps. While this strategy established India as a respected player in the global space market, it has begun to show diminishing returns in today's rapidly evolving landscape.

Diminishing Cost Advantage: For years, ISRO enjoyed a significant cost advantage in the satellite launch market. However, this edge has been dramatically eroded by SpaceX's reusable rocket technology. While ISRO focuses on optimizing existing expendable-rocket designs, SpaceX's Falcon 9 boosters—which can be launched, recovered and reused multiple times—have fundamentally transformed launch economics. The baseline cost of placing a kilogram into orbit with SpaceX is estimated at $5000, approximately one-tenth of previous industry standards. By contrast, analysts suggest ISRO's costs are now four to five times higher than SpaceX's.

Scale Limitations: ISRO's launch cadence remains limited to approximately four missions annually, while SpaceX conducts dozens of launches per year. This disparity creates a significant scale disadvantage for ISRO, making it difficult to amortize fixed costs across missions and achieve economies of scale in manufacturing and operations.

Reinventing ISRO

For ISRO to maintain its relevance in this transformed landscape, it must evolve its approach to LeanSpark, not by abandoning jugaad principles, but by applying them in more sophisticated and strategic ways.

Private Sector Engagement: A key element of ISRO's adaptation strategy involves embracing collaboration with India's growing private space sector. In September 2022, NewSpace India Limited contracted with a Hindustan Aeronautics Limited and Larsen & Toubro consortium to produce five PSLV-XL launch vehicles, marking a significant shift towards industrial participation in rocket production.

This approach mirrors successful models in the United States, where NASA's commercial partnerships with companies like SpaceX have revitalized American space capabilities. By leveraging private-sector efficiency and investment, ISRO can potentially increase its launch cadence and focus its own resources on the research and development of next-generation technologies.

From Incremental to Disruptive Innovation: While ISRO has excelled at incremental improvements, competing in today's space market requires more disruptive approaches. The organization must balance its tradition of frugality with targeted investments in technologies that can fundamentally change its cost structure and capabilities.

Going forward, there are several potential areas for ISRO to focus on, including:

Reusable Launch Systems: While developing fully reusable rockets like SpaceX's would require substantial investment, ISRO could pursue intermediate approaches that involve recovering and reusing the most expensive components.

Advanced Manufacturing: Adopting techniques like 3D printing and automated assembly could reduce production costs and increase the rate of rocket production.

In-Space Propulsion: Developing more efficient propulsion systems could enable ISRO to continue offering cost-effective solutions for missions beyond Earth orbit.

A Global Model for Space Exploration

ISRO's journey shows that while its early cost-effective approaches were highly effective, the organization needs to evolve as technology advances and global competition increases. The future of innovation in the space sector may lie in a blended model one that brings together smart resource use, LeanSpark's structured and scalable methods, focused investments in breakthrough technologies and stronger public–private partnerships.

This shift is not about letting go of India's original mindset of doing more with less, but about building on it. ISRO's success offers a powerful example for other sectors, both in India and globally, showing how constraints can spark new thinking. LeanSpark could help tackle some of the world's toughest challenges. It has the potential to reshape how high-tech industries approach innovation globally. As ISRO continues to reach for the stars, it inspires not just a nation, but the world, proving that with ingenuity and perseverance, even the sky is not the limit.

Conclusion

Not Just a Method, but a Movement

Beyond a method or a mindset, LeanSpark is also a movement. This book draws from the deep well of Indian ingenuity, evolving the spirit of jugaad into a disciplined, technology-powered framework for building solutions that are frugal, scalable and sustainable.

The New Global Gauntlet

India's moment is defined not just by its own aspirations, but by the gauntlet thrown down by the rest of the world. Western models that are capital-intensive, resource-heavy and often exclusive are increasingly unsuited to an era of climate crisis, inequality and finite resources. But the challenge is no longer only from the West. China, too, has rewritten the rules of innovation, building global giants like DJI in drones, BYD in electric vehicles, and DeepSeek in artificial intelligence. China's playbook is state-led, scale-driven and relentless in execution. It has set a new benchmark for what is possible from the Global South.

For India, the challenge is not just to catch up, but to leap ahead, by building its own DeepSeeks, DJIs and BYDs, not as copycats but as companies that reflect India's unique strengths and realities. India's path will not, and should not, be a mirror image of China's. Where China leverages centralized scale, India's strength lies in decentralized diversity. Where China's innovation is often top-down, India's is bottom-up, built on the creative energy of millions of entrepreneurs, engineers and communities.

LeanSpark offers India a way to take on China and the West at their own game, but on Indian terms. It's about building world-class enterprises in sectors where India has natural advantages: digital public infrastructure, affordable healthcare, inclusive fintech, frugal AI, clean energy and education. It's about compensating for weaknesses in capital, infrastructure and scale, with ingenuity, adaptability and a relentless focus on affordability and access.

Above all, the LeanSpark movement is a call to draw on India's biggest resource: its people, especially its youth; their curiosity and grit; and their quiet refusal to accept the way things are.

India's Hidden Superpower

But perhaps India's greatest strength isn't just its size or its young population. Perhaps it's something quieter and often overlooked: the ability to innovate under constraint. To work with what's at hand.

We've seen this play out across sectors. Chetan Maini reimagined electric mobility before it was cool. Nandan Nilekani and Vivek Raghavan helped build the rails of digital identity. Deepthi Bopaiah is transforming sports access for underprivileged youth. Rahat Kulshreshtha turned a drone into a sporting tool. Arjun Arunachalam built an MRI machine on a shoestring budget.

And it's not just people. It's also systems. India's digital public infrastructure, like Aadhaar, UPI and ONDC, have become the backbone of inclusive innovation. No other country has a stack like this. It allows start-ups and governments to co-create solutions that are affordable *and* ambitious.

While we don't have China's state-led playbook or Silicon Valley's capital firepower, we have something else. An open, messy, wonderfully chaotic marketplace of ideas. A culture wired to do more with less. And the courage to try, fail and try again. This is what LeanSpark thrives on. It may not offer perfection, but it does promise progress.

LeanSpark is a response not just to China or the West, but to the world's shared challenges of climate change, inequality and the need for scale without waste. The future won't belong to those who spend the most, but to those who use frugal ingenuity to design for everyone.

A Movement for All

LeanSpark is not reserved for entrepreneurs or policymakers. It's for everyone. It's for the student in a rural school with a smartphone and a dream. For the engineer in a city start-up trying to solve for the next billion users. For the community leader tackling problems with limited resources but boundless commitment. For the corporate leader trying to steer a large organization towards greater agility and impact. LeanSpark invites all of us to view constraints not as limitations, but as creative starting points.

What makes this movement powerful are its core principles, what we've come to define as the LeanSpark attributes:

Lean execution *encourages speed, experimentation and learning from failure without the need for massive resources.*

Purposeful simplicity *is about cutting through the noise, focusing on what truly matters and building only what is essential.*

Adaptive scalability *ensures that solutions are flexible enough to grow and evolve across different geographies, user groups and constraints.*

Systemic sustainability *is about solving problems at the root, with long-term impact, minimal waste and an inclusive lens.*

This book is both a chronicle of these ideas and a call to action. The stories and case studies you've read show what becomes possible when frugal ingenuity is paired with structure, technology and clear purpose. They demonstrate that innovation doesn't need to wait for ideal conditions or unlimited capital. It can begin now, with what we have, where we are.

LeanSpark is an evolving practice, one that belongs to anyone willing to start.

LeanSpark Toolkit
The Frugal Innovation Canvas

The Frugal Innovation Canvas (FIC) is your blueprint for doing more with less, and for doing it at scale. Rooted in the principles of LeanSpark, this canvas is not just a planning tool; it puts your mindset into motion. The FIC is inspired from the four core attributes of LeanSpark: lean execution, purposeful simplicity, adaptive scalability and systemic sustainability. Together, they shape the way innovators build under constraint, with a focus on how to survive and thrive.

This canvas helps you break down ideas into practical steps, identify the core problem, understand your audience, embrace constraints and craft lean solutions. From key resources to revenue models and channels of delivery, each box nudges you to innovate under real-world pressures. Whether you're a start-up founder, social entrepreneur or corporate leader, this is your tool for turning limitations into launch pads.

We've applied the FIC with many founders at universities like Cambridge and Ashoka. It's helped them make their ideas frugal, build resilience into their operations and design for scale without excess. In our classrooms, incubators and workshops, we've seen how the FIC sparks creativity amongst constraints. It forces hard choices. But in doing so, it unlocks something powerful: a path to scale, growth without waste and innovation without privilege.

But before we walk you through the canvas, here's a short story.

Ecobricks, today a worldwide phenomenon, is said to have begun in the Philippines. In 2010, Russel Maiser, a Canadian artist, was travelling across the country with his girlfriend to meet her family. The meeting did not go well; midway, his girlfriend dumped Russel and flew back to Paris. A heartbroken Russel continued his travels, seeking wisdom for his art from indigenous people.

Russel was intrigued that in the village where he lived, despite the waste all around, the local language had no word for trash. For them everything had value. They would frequently use the word *'ayyew'* which meant that an item when discarded could be recycled and transformed into something else.

One day Russel packed small plastic pieces and sand into plastic bottles and used these as bricks to create a garden. He shared this idea with the local school where children made their own plastic Ecobricks. Word spread and the school superintendent had 200 schools follow this practice. In 2013 Russel set up a website and soon began to hear from other people who were independently making bricks from waste. He connected with Ecobrickers around the world, making it a worldwide movement. Something that was considered waste with little or no commercial value had, in a LeanSpark moment, become useful while also solving a serious environmental problem.

In India Ecobricks are used in road construction. They are also used in making paver tiles and interlocking blocks that are used for pathways and sideways. The National Highway Authority of India found that using recycled material like plastics and fly ash, besides solving the problem of waste and pollution, makes roads stronger and more weather resistant.

The Ecobricks story is a vivid demonstration of how the FIC comes to life. The project starts with a clear customer segment—communities struggling with plastic pollution—and identifies the core problem of waste management. By embracing local constraints (limited municipal recycling, scarce building materials), Ecobricks leverages available resources (discarded plastic bottles and wrappers) and delivers a frugal solution (affordable, durable construction material). The entire journey, from problem identification to impact, can be mapped step-by-step on the canvas, offering a replicable model for other grassroots innovations.

But Ecobricks is not just an isolated act of ingenuity; it is a blueprint for how anyone, anywhere, can use the FIC to turn local problems into scalable solutions that serve both people and the planet.

Using the FIC

Let's now examine the FIC and understand the boxes in the framework in more detail. Be aware though that there is no particular order to filling them in. In fact, you may go from one box to another and then to a third box before finding your way back to where you started. The advantage of the FIC is that you can see the entire plan in one go and visualize how a change in one box impacts others.

Customer Segment	Core Problem	Constraints
Who is the customer or community being served?	What are the challenges they currently face?	What is the compelling limitation you need to work with?

Frugal Solution

What value does your product or service deliver?
How is the new business model different from the current one?

Key Resources	Revenue Model	Channels
What do you need to make this work in terms of people, material, tools or partnerships?	How will you generate income and make it sustainable?	How will you reach your customers?

Impact

How have customers lives improved with this solution
In what way does it differ from existing alternatives consumer have?

Customer Segment

Who are your most important customers?
How old are they and where do they live?
What do they earn?
How will they interact with your product or service?

Your target could be an existing customer segment currently being served by a suboptimal solution. This could be one that either doesn't fully solve their problem or over-delivers in ways that add unnecessary cost and complexity. Frugal innovation shines brightest when it identifies such gaps, especially for segments that are cost-conscious and prioritize affordability, functionality, ease of use, etc.

These customers may include individuals with financial constraints, but increasingly, they may also include those who are simply mindful about value. They don't want clutter. They want essentials done well. For example, Mukesh (author) wears a smartwatch all the time. He has disabled every feature except step-tracking and sleep-monitoring. That's all he needs. And that's true for many users today who seek intentional minimalism.

The same ethos drives demand for frugal innovations like low-cost mobile phones, compact diagnostic tools like handheld ultrasounds in rural India or affordable prosthetic limbs designed for mass production. In Kenya and much of sub-Saharan Africa, M-Pesa didn't just disrupt the banking sector, it redefined access for millions who had been underbanked or excluded entirely. It was functional and it worked.

When Chetan Maini (Chapter 1.2) launched the Reva electric car, he wasn't targeting the luxury EV market. He focused instead on urban commuters in India looking for an economical, sustainable mobility solution. These were users who didn't want horsepower or cutting-edge design; they wanted low-cost, clean, city-friendly commuting. And by understanding this specific need, Maini designed a car that was practical, compact and revolutionary in its frugality.

Similarly, BigBasket's founders (Chapter 1.3) zeroed in on busy urban households, dual-income families, working professionals and time-starved individuals. These customers didn't need gourmet or imported items. They needed vegetables delivered on time, fresh groceries without hassle and reliability over razzle-dazzle. Traditional kirana stores and supermarkets were missing that mark. BigBasket didn't invent online groceries, they refined the service for a customer segment long overlooked.

All these innovators saw not just *gaps* in the market but understood the mindset of the people. They listened carefully, stripped away the noise and built products that fit. Frugal innovation begins with deep empathy and sharp focus on who you're really serving.

Core Problem

What does the customer actually need?
Are they able to articulate it?
How can you draw the customer to your product or service?

This is the anchor of any frugal innovation effort. It's not just what's broken, it's about what's *missing*. What's being poorly addressed. What's been over-engineered for the few or entirely overlooked by traditional approaches. This is the fundamental challenge you are trying to solve, often in a way that's radically more accessible, affordable and efficient than existing options.

To define the core problem well, you need to go beyond surface symptoms. You need to empathize with your user deeply, not just what they say they want, but what they actually need. Frugal innovators zero in on an essential need.

Identifying the core problem means asking hard questions: Why hasn't this been solved yet? Who's been left out? What assumptions are baked into current solutions? Why haven't they scaled? What are the cost, infrastructure or cultural barriers?

For instance, the lack of clean drinking water isn't just about supply, it's about access to low-cost filtration in rural or low-income areas. Responses like gravity-based water purifiers that don't require electricity solve this in a simple yet powerful way. Similarly, portable toilets that don't use water address sanitation in regions where plumbing is non-existent or unreliable.

Then there's the issue of education where millions of students at the bottom of the pyramid (BoP) are eager to learn but lack access to quality teachers or structured content. Online platforms designed with low bandwidth, mobile-first interfaces and vernacular content have emerged as frugal, scalable solutions. Or take healthcare. Incubators like the portable infant warmer have saved premature babies in areas without access to neonatal ICUs by asking 'What's the *minimum* needed to keep a baby warm safely?'

We've seen this play out across sectors. GoSports Foundation, led by Deepthi Bopaiah (Chapter 3.1), realized that India wasn't lacking talent. Athletes were dropping out not for lack of potential, but because there was no support system beyond the spotlight. Their core problem? A broken pipeline between the potential and the podium.

For Nandan Nilekani, Vivek Raghavan and the Aadhaar team (Chapter 3.2), the challenge was existential: Over a billion Indians had no universal, verifiable identity. That meant no bank accounts, no subsidies, no access to the digital economy. The core problem was scale and inclusion.

At its best, identifying the core problem forces innovators to zoom in on the *people* behind the problem. At this stage just focus on identifying the problem and not the solution. It invites you to simplify and maybe just reframe the problem statement.

Constraints

If current solutions exist what is limiting their growth?
Are there constraints due to income, geography, education or others that you need to discover?
Are these constraints hard (non-negotiable) or soft (can we worked around) in nature?

Constraints need not be roadblocks, they can be invitations to think differently and resourcefully. In the world of frugal innovation, constraints are opportunities for breakthrough thinking. In fact, many of the most game-changing solutions have emerged *not despite* constraints, but *because of them*.

To navigate constraints effectively, you need an entrepreneurial mindset that is grounded in critical thinking. This means refusing to accept that limited budgets, infrastructure or systems are dead ends.

We encounter constraints in everyday life too. Can you plan your day while staying flexible with unexpected curveballs? Can you lead a team while also being approachable and empathetic? Can you pursue a career without compromising your values or personal life? We do this dance daily, adjusting, improvising and rebalancing.

Take Toyota, for instance. Its paradoxical expectations of employees are legendary:

- Be frugal even when spending large sums
- Be efficient yet maintain redundancy
- Dissent respectfully while working within a hierarchy

These contradictions are baked into the culture because Toyota understands that resilience lives in tension. That innovation often requires pulling from opposite directions at once.

When Abhinay Choudhari launched BigBasket (Chapter 1.3), he ran headfirst into India's logistical chaos: unpredictable supply chains, power outages and the notorious 'last mile' delivery gap. Instead of seeing these as deal-breakers, his team hacked around them. They used open-source tech to keep costs low, built custom vans with cold storage, and created a hub-and-spoke model suited to Indian cities. The very obstacles that threatened to kill the idea became its competitive edge.

Similarly, ISRO's journey (Chapter 3.4) reads like a masterclass in constraint-driven ingenuity. Locked out of international collaborations. Underfunded compared to NASA. Tasked with ambitions that far exceeded its budget. And yet, it built and launched the Mars Orbiter Mission for less money than it takes to make a Hollywood movie. Their mantra: if you can't import the best, build what you need locally, and make it work.

A constraint forces focus. It sharpens priorities. It exposes inefficiencies. Once you stop chasing the perfect conditions and start solving with *what is*, you begin to build solutions that are relevant.

Frugal Solution

Is this the most efficient way to address your customers' problem?
Is this the most resource-efficient way to address your customers' problem?
Will economies of scale or scope make your product or service cheaper and more widely used?

This is the *heart* of the FIC. The part where mindset matters most. It begins with understanding that constraints are often wrapped in paradoxes, and that progress doesn't come from choosing one side of a contradiction, but from holding both in tension. To design frugally, you must embrace a paradoxical mindset: one that sees through binary thinking and acknowledges that opposites can not only coexist but actually fuel innovation.

This isn't just abstract theory. It's how the best of art, science and human experience operates. Artists have long played with paradoxes. Think of Picasso, whose paintings carry both light and dark, abstraction and realism, fragmentation and unity. In music, dissonance creates emotional depth; silence and sound are equal parts of the melody. In literature, contradiction often reveals the deeper truth.

Even life itself is a paradox. Breathing involves simultaneous opposites—inhale and exhale, expansion and contraction. You need both to live. Or consider what Niels Bohr, the Nobel-winning physicist, once said: 'How wonderful that we have met with a paradox. Now we have some hope of making progress.'

Think of a passenger on a moving train who is both at rest and in motion at the same time. Robert Oppenheimer, another scientific giant, once posed the classic riddle to his students: Is light a particle or a wave? The answer? Both. A landmark study of twenty-two Nobel laureates found that their biggest breakthroughs emerged when they were able to hold multiple opposites in their minds at once.

This kind of thinking is crucial in frugal innovation. Because frugal solutions often require you to:

- Add value while slashing costs
- Deliver high quality with minimal resources
- Design for simplicity while solving complex problems
- Scale while staying grounded in local context

That's the LeanSpark way: flipping constraints into strengths, and turning either-or into both-and.

Rahat (Chapter 1.1) wanted to build a world-class player-tracking system for live sports, but without the million-dollar gear used by global broadcasters. The solution was the Quidich Tracker, an AI-driven system built using affordable, repurposed hardware, laser-focused on just the essentials. That was the paradox: delivering elite performance on a shoestring budget.

Remember The ePlane Company (Chapter 1.1) which is building flying taxis for India's dense cities? Instead of designing from scratch with shiny, expensive tech, they adapted existing aircraft components and reimagined logistics around rooftop landings to avoid the need for new airports or runways. Innovation through limitation.

Frugal innovation thrives in these contradictions. It invites us to challenge either/or thinking. So, when faced with a paradox, don't shy away. Because within that tension lies your most potent creative spark.

Key Resources

What resources do you require to support your

- *Value proposition*
- *Distribution channels*
- *Customer relationships*
- *Revenue streams*

Resources come in many forms. Some obvious, others invisible until you really start looking. Financial capital is the one everyone talks about. But just as critical are human capital (your people and skills), intellectual capital (your knowledge, IP or design thinking) and often the most undervalued of all: time. In frugal innovation, the art lies in recognizing the true value of each resource and using it with care. Every unit wasted, whether it's money, hours or effort, adds cost, complexity and drag.

The Japanese have a powerful term for this: '*mottainai*'. It loosely translates to 'don't be wasteful', but its roots run deeper into Buddhist and Shinto philosophies, and more recently, into the DNA of lean manufacturing. Mottainai isn't just about saving money: it's about respecting the

Channels

What channels do my customers prefer?
Which of them works best and is the most cost-efficient?
Are there some unconventional distribution channels that are not currently being used?

In this box, you'll identify the smartest, simplest and most cost-effective way to reach your user. It's about maximizing reach with minimal friction. Frugal innovators know that great solutions fail if they don't reach the right people at the right time. So, the question is, how can you get there without breaking the bank?

Thanks to technologies like AI, mobile networks, cloud computing and 3D printing, the landscape of distribution and delivery has radically changed. What once required massive infrastructure and capital can now be achieved with a smartphone and a signal. But technology alone isn't enough. You also need to think locally, culturally, logistically and socially.

That means exploring unconventional distribution models:

- Partnering with NGOs, self-help groups or public health workers
- Using mobile showrooms or pop-up kiosks that travel to remote areas
- Training local youth or village girls as entrepreneurs and last-mile agents
- Embedding your product within existing community rituals or micro-markets

energy, people and intention behind everything we use. This mindset lies at the core of LeanSpark: not parsimony, but purposeful use.

Frugal innovation overlaps beautifully with the effectuation principle of 'means at hand', proposed by Saras Sarasvathy. You don't wait for the perfect conditions or ideal funding. You begin with what you already have. You ask three deceptively simple questions:

- Who am I?
- What do I know?
- Whom do I know?

From there, you start building. As you move forward, you'll discover unexpected allies, serendipitous turns and new capabilities. Partnerships (explored more under channels) will emerge not just from business plans but from real, lived interactions.

Take Quidich Innovation Labs (Chapter 1.1). They didn't wait for a massive team or top-tier broadcast equipment. They started with a small, multidisciplinary crew, coders, camera operators, engineers and repurposed off-the-shelf drones to create a first-of-its-kind aerial tracking system for live sports.

Chai Point's (Chapter 1.3) success wasn't built on sprawling outlets or expensive barista training. Their core resources were standardized tea recipes, compact store formats and an army of IoT-enabled Chai Cubes that kept quality high and overheads low. This thoughtful use of process and automation allowed them to scale fast without bloated costs.

In frugal innovation, every resource is a lever. You don't need more, you need to be *sharp*. Because when you respect your resources, your innovation respects the people it serves.

Revenue Model

Who will bear the cost of the product or service?
Is this sustainable over the long run?

For a frugal solution to be sustainable, you'll need to be creative not only in product design and delivery but also in how value is captured. You're not just selling a product or a service, you're designing a system that pays for itself, adapts and scales.

This may mean rethinking ownership. Can your solution be delivered through leasing or subscription rather than full purchase? Can it involve modular design, so users can upgrade or repair rather than replace? Can you create pricing tiers or cross-subsidization models, where those who can afford to pay more indirectly support access for those who can't?

A great example is the Aravind Eye Care System, which has become a global benchmark for sustainable frugal innovation. Aravind doesn't just offer low-cost, high-quality eye care, it has reimagined its entire business model. Through massive volume (thousands of surgeries per day), cross-subsidization (wealthier patients pay more, allowing the poor to be treated for free or at minimal cost) and vertical integration (manufacturing their own lenses), Aravind has built a model that is both impactful and self-sustaining. Their revenue model is as innovative as their clinical work.

GoSports Foundation (Chapter 3.1) built a high-impact athlete support system. But how di it? Not through ticket sales or government ha by strategically aligning with CSR mandates. T corporates that supporting athletes could be measurable form of social impact. The result: a s of CSR funding that ensured long-term support without chasing short-term revenue.

Chai Point (Chapter 1.3) cracked the code revenue in a hyper-competitive F&B space. Beyon ins at retail outlets, they locked in corporate offices consistent supply of quality tea. Their IoT-enable ensured smooth operations and tracking, creati predictable revenue stream. This diversification pi from footfall fluctuations and allowed them to pla

When building your revenue model for a fruga ask:

- Can users pay in smaller chunks: per us per outcome?
- Can you generate non-user revenue thro partners and platforms?
- Can your pricing *incentivize scale* witho inclusion?

Remember: Frugality isn't about charging le creating value *efficiently* and then designing a v that value that aligns with the user's reality. Beca a frugal solution that doesn't earn enough to sus a solution at all.

energy, people and intention behind everything we use. This mindset lies at the core of LeanSpark: not parsimony, but purposeful use.

Frugal innovation overlaps beautifully with the effectuation principle of 'means at hand', proposed by Saras Sarasvathy. You don't wait for the perfect conditions or ideal funding. You begin with what you already have. You ask three deceptively simple questions:

- Who am I?
- What do I know?
- Whom do I know?

From there, you start building. As you move forward, you'll discover unexpected allies, serendipitous turns and new capabilities. Partnerships (explored more under channels) will emerge not just from business plans but from real, lived interactions.

Take Quidich Innovation Labs (Chapter 1.1). They didn't wait for a massive team or top-tier broadcast equipment. They started with a small, multidisciplinary crew, coders, camera operators, engineers and repurposed off-the-shelf drones to create a first-of-its-kind aerial tracking system for live sports.

Chai Point's (Chapter 1.3) success wasn't built on sprawling outlets or expensive barista training. Their core resources were standardized tea recipes, compact store formats and an army of IoT-enabled Chai Cubes that kept quality high and overheads low. This thoughtful use of process and automation allowed them to scale fast without bloated costs.

In frugal innovation, every resource is a lever. You don't need more, you need to be *sharp*. Because when you respect your resources, your innovation respects the people it serves.

Revenue Model

Who will bear the cost of the product or service?
Is this sustainable over the long run?

For a frugal solution to be sustainable, you'll need to be creative not only in product design and delivery but also in how value is captured. You're not just selling a product or a service, you're designing a system that pays for itself, adapts and scales.

This may mean rethinking ownership. Can your solution be delivered through leasing or subscription rather than full purchase? Can it involve modular design, so users can upgrade or repair rather than replace? Can you create pricing tiers or cross-subsidization models, where those who can afford to pay more indirectly support access for those who can't?

A great example is the Aravind Eye Care System, which has become a global benchmark for sustainable frugal innovation. Aravind doesn't just offer low-cost, high-quality eye care, it has reimagined its entire business model. Through massive volume (thousands of surgeries per day), cross-subsidization (wealthier patients pay more, allowing the poor to be treated for free or at minimal cost) and vertical integration (manufacturing their own lenses), Aravind has built a model that is both impactful and self-sustaining. Their revenue model is as innovative as their clinical work.

GoSports Foundation (Chapter 3.1) built a frugal but high-impact athlete support system. But how did they fund it? Not through ticket sales or government handouts, but by strategically aligning with CSR mandates. They showed corporates that supporting athletes could be a powerful, measurable form of social impact. The result: a steady stream of CSR funding that ensured long-term support for players, without chasing short-term revenue.

Chai Point (Chapter 1.3) cracked the code of recurring revenue in a hyper-competitive F&B space. Beyond daily walk-ins at retail outlets, they locked in corporate offices that needed a consistent supply of quality tea. Their IoT-enabled Chai Cubes ensured smooth operations and tracking, creating a robust, predictable revenue stream. This diversification protected them from footfall fluctuations and allowed them to plan for scale.

When building your revenue model for a frugal innovation, ask:

- Can users pay in smaller chunks: per use, per month, per outcome?
- Can you generate non-user revenue through sponsors, partners and platforms?
- Can your pricing *incentivize scale* without sacrificing inclusion?

Remember: Frugality isn't about charging less. It's about creating value *efficiently* and then designing a way to capture that value that aligns with the user's reality. Because in the end, a frugal solution that doesn't earn enough to sustain itself isn't a solution at all.

Channels

What channels do my customers prefer?
Which of them works best and is the most cost-efficient?
Are there some unconventional distribution channels that are not currently being used?

In this box, you'll identify the smartest, simplest and most cost-effective way to reach your user. It's about maximizing reach with minimal friction. Frugal innovators know that great solutions fail if they don't reach the right people at the right time. So, the question is, how can you get there without breaking the bank?

Thanks to technologies like AI, mobile networks, cloud computing and 3D printing, the landscape of distribution and delivery has radically changed. What once required massive infrastructure and capital can now be achieved with a smartphone and a signal. But technology alone isn't enough. You also need to think locally, culturally, logistically and socially.

That means exploring unconventional distribution models:

- Partnering with NGOs, self-help groups or public health workers
- Using mobile showrooms or pop-up kiosks that travel to remote areas
- Training local youth or village girls as entrepreneurs and last-mile agents
- Embedding your product within existing community rituals or micro-markets

- Leveraging community radio, WhatsApp groups or even folk theatre to spread awareness

LaundryMate, built by Abhinay Choudhari (Chapter 1.3), didn't follow the traditional dry-cleaning route. It reimagined the entire delivery model. Customers ordered pickups digitally, laundry was processed in central hubs, and deliveries were made during off-peak night hours to avoid traffic and save time. A smooth, tech-enabled operation that stayed lean, fast and affordable.

Chai Point (Chapter 1.3) mastered a dual-channel approach. On one hand, they set up outlets in high-footfall areas like tech parks, metro stations and airports, where the cost of acquiring a customer was low. On the other, they used digital ordering platforms, including a robust app and corporate dashboards to service enterprise clients and repeat orders.

When filling this box, ask:

- Where are my customers already going?
- Who already has access to them, and can I partner instead of build?
- What low-cost or high-trust networks can I plug into?
- Is there a tech layer I can add that reduces dependency on physical infrastructure?

Sometimes the best channel is right in front of you. It might be the kirana store auntie who knows everyone who lives on your lane. It might be a WhatsApp group for a school PTA. It might be the digital wallet app already on every phone.

Reach doesn't have to be expensive. But it does have to be intentional.

Impact

What is the impact you are seeking at the individual and societal level? Can this be scaled and replicated?

This box represents not only the direct impact on the customer, but the larger, systemic effect your product or service could have on society. The impact you create could be economic, by generating livelihoods or enabling small businesses. It could be environmental, by using fewer natural resources, reducing waste or offering green alternatives. It could be social, by empowering women, bridging education gaps or making culture more accessible. In emerging markets especially, frugal innovation becomes a tool for transformation. Every unit sold, every person served, has the potential to ripple outward and uplift communities.

Take, for example, water filtration systems that don't need electricity. Or renewable energy kits that power homes in off-grid villages. Or low-cost diagnostic tools that let frontline health workers screen for diseases in remote areas. These aren't just products; they're platforms for equity.

Consider the case of menstrual hygiene. For years, menstrual pads were made from expensive and often inaccessible materials—cotton, plastic, even compressed wood. In many parts of the world, this meant that millions of women and girls simply had no reliable solution. But a team led by Manu Prakash at Stanford University looked at this problem through a frugal lens. They turned to the sisal plant, a rugged, fibrous plant long used by villages in Central America and Africa to make rope. Through a process called delignification, they were able to transform its long leaves into a fluffy, absorbent material that performs remarkably well as a menstrual pad. A local solution to solve a global problem.

Cultural impact matters too. The Jaipur Literature Festival, led by Sanjoy Roy (Chapter 2.1), changed the way people access the arts. By keeping entry free and partnering strategically to scale, it created a democratic space for conversation, creativity and storytelling, without the usual barriers of cost, credentials or language. This is frugal innovation in a cultural avatar, proving you don't need massive budgets to create massive movements.

In education, Teach For India, inspired by Shaheen Mistri (Chapter 2.4), goes beyond just measuring the number of teaching fellows placed in classrooms. It tracks the ripple effects on students, schools and eventually, systems. Many fellows go on to start NGOs, influence policy or lead schools, amplifying the original impact through layers of change.

When you fill this box, go beyond metrics like sales or clicks. Ask: What larger problem is my product contributing to solving? Who else benefits when the direct user benefits? How might this innovation affect equity, agency and resilience in the long run?

Frugal innovations, when done right, punch above their weight. And they often become catalysts for change for entire communities and systems.

That's the kind of impact this canvas helps you build towards.

Bringing It All Together: Assembling the Canvas

Just as Ecobricks turned a local waste problem into a global movement, the FIC offers a structured way for entrepreneurs and change-makers to identify needs, work with constraints and deliver scalable impact, whether in technology, healthcare, education or the arts.

Every story in this book, from Quidich's drones to BigBasket's grocery revolution, can be mapped onto the canvas, showing how LeanSpark thinking turns limitations into launch pads for lasting change.

We've used this canvas to guide hundreds of entrepreneurs from first-time founders in dorm rooms to experienced professionals pivoting toward more sustainable models. Whether it was an ed-tech start-up figuring out how to deliver learning in no-internet zones, or a healthcare venture redesigning diagnostic tools to reach Tier 3 cities, the FIC became their playbook. Not just for ideation, but for frugalizing their business models, simplifying their operations and aligning with what really matters: impact, affordability and adaptability.

LeanSpark is not a limitation. It's a liberation. And the canvas is your launch pad.

Customer Segment	Core Problem	Constraints
Frugal Solution		
Key Resources	Revenue Model	Channels
Impact		

Use this blank canvas to frugalize your ideas

Epilogue

In the End, a Beginning

We didn't set out to write a theory.
We set out to understand a feeling.

That spark in a young founder's eyes.
A hacked-together prototype solving a local problem.
The restless energy in classrooms, labs and factory floors.
That itch to fix what feels broken, but to do it differently.
What ignited this wasn't access to capital or Ivy League polish.
It was the refusal to be limited by constraint.

This book grew out of that feeling.
Out of hundreds of stories.
Late-night zoom calls across three time zones.
Trips to Cambridge and Ashoka.
Scribbled notes on Post-its and envelopes.

This book grew out of a belief that India's way of solving problems deserves to be celebrated, not apologized for.

LeanSpark is what we chose to call it.
But really, it's a name for something deeper.
An instinct. A kind of energy.
To make do with less. To make it better.
But most importantly, to make it last.

If you're reading this, you're already part of that feeling.
Whether you're a creator, a teacher, a policymaker or someone quietly shaping your corner of the world.

LeanSpark isn't just for India.
It's for any place where resources are tight, challenges are urgent and people are hungry to make a difference.

And isn't that the world we live in today?

The question isn't: Do you have enough?
It's: What will you do with what you've got?
Make a beginning. The spark is already there.
Lean into it.

—Jaideep, Priyank and Mukesh

Acknowledgements

'Houston, we have a problem.'

With these five words, an ordinary space mission changed into a race to solve what seemed an impossible challenge. A tank on board Apollo 13 had exploded, forcing the astronauts to retreat to the lunar module with its limited oxygen supply. All they had available to them were the tools on board and their own ingenuity.

Speed, focus and smart thinking was their lifeline—all elements of LeanSpark.

This book was not built in a research lab. It was grown in the wild. In crowded classrooms and campus cafés. Through long debates, short deadlines and occasional existential crises. It is the sum of many sparks, generously shared by friends, colleagues, mentors and strangers who became part of this journey.

To the innovators, entrepreneurs, policymakers, students and dreamers we interviewed: thank you for opening your doors and your minds. Your stories gave this book its heartbeat.

A big thank you to Avnie Garg and Nikhil Sud, our very first partners on this journey. When this *book* was just an idea, they helped shape it into something real. Avnie, as a teaching associate, and Nikhil, who teaches product management at Ashoka, brought energy, clarity and heart. They helped us map the book, brainstormed ideas, connected us to people and transcribed what felt like a million interviews. We wouldn't have gotten off the ground without them.

Here's a toast to the fantastic team at Penguin Random House India, led by our dear friend Gaurav Shrinagesh. Radhika Marwah, thank you for believing in *LeanSpark* before it had a name. Your sharp eye, gentle nudges and steady guidance helped the book come into being. Congratulations on your little one; she's probably been absorbing frugal innovation lessons even before she arrived. Rinku Paul, thank you for being our rock during the crunch phase; your calm made all the difference. Manoj Satti and his brilliant team brought their A-game to marketing and sales. We're truly grateful. And to Sanjiv Gupta, another dear friend from Penguin, who's since moved on to another organization, but backed us at every step: thank you for everything.

It takes a village to write a book. We're grateful to friends from Cambridge Judge Business School who stepped in and supported in so many ways—Serish Gandikota, Marvin Fernandes, Elisabetta Osta, Suyash Bhatt and Kal Sandhu. Thank you for being there.

A very special shout-out to Alba Prabhu Carreres. All of sixteen, she volunteered to help with the citations, and we couldn't be more grateful.

To our colleagues at Ashoka University, especially at the Centre for Entrepreneurship, thank you for creating a space where ideas are tested, challenged and nurtured. Ekanto and Sagar, your commitment kept us moving. Vice Chancellor Somak Raychaudhury, Chairman Pramath Raj Sinha and Chairman Emeritus Ashish Dhawan, thank you for being steady supporters and mentors throughout our journey.

To our students at Cambridge, Ashoka and IIM Ahmedabad, you keep surprising us. Thank you for showing us what frugal, fearless innovation looks like. And finally, to everyone who believes big change doesn't need big budgets. That simplicity is a superpower. That doing more with less isn't a compromise, it's a craft.

This book is for you.

Jaideep Prabhu

I am grateful to my wife and children for giving me the space to meet the demands of writing this book. My colleagues at Cambridge Judge Business School deserve thanks for fostering a culture of inquiry and risk-taking, enabling me to pursue ideas that began as sparks and grew into sustained research. I would like to thank C.K. Prahalad, R.A. Mashelkar, Nandan Nilekani, Yusuf Hamied and Fazle Hasan Abed for their inspiration over the years.

Above all, I am indebted to my co-authors, Priyank and Mukesh, whose energy, insight and tenacity made *LeanSpark* a reality. Our countless conversations in Ashoka's classrooms, Cambridge's cafés and online became the foundation for what you now read. This book is a testament to their boundless curiosity, goodwill and belief that together we can make a difference, no matter what the constraints.

Priyank Narayan

To my wife Pooja for surviving the lost weekends, dinner-table rants about frugal and the occasional monologue on systemic sustainability (sorry!). Your patience and belief kept this going. To my parents, in-laws and the whole gang: thank you for cheering me on, feeding me, buying me that drink and pretending to understand what LeanSpark means. ☺

To my rockstars, Avyaan and Aran who are always curious, always asking, 'Why not?' This book is for you. May you carry the spark in everything you build, break and reimagine. Stay wild.

And finally, my co-conspirators, Jaideep and Mukesh, thank you for the madness and the method. We argued, riffed, laughed, rewrote and sometimes just stared at the white board. But we made it. Wouldn't want to do this with anyone else.

Mukesh Sud

It should not require mentioning but it does.

Thanks to my wife Neera and children who allow me to be part of such an adventurous project like *LeanSpark*. For reasons I have not been able to figure out, they let me indulge in my latest fascination and pursue it till I find a new one. After years in academia, where I was constantly reporting my research output in ABDC journals, these are fun projects that I enjoy doing.

The real appreciation though is to Jaideep and Priyank. Jaideep for laughing through all the ribbing I do about our past professional association. And Priyank who has tolerated my constant bullying over the years.

They are both real friends.

Notes and Selected References

As authors rooted in both practice and academia, we've tried to balance the spark of real-world stories with the rigour of research. Many of the insights in this book come from our own lived experiences, those of the innovators we met and the students we've taught.

Wherever possible, we've grounded these ideas in published research, data and frameworks that help explain *why* something worked. They're part of a larger conversation between theory and action; and between academia and the real world.

And in the spirit of transparency: yes, we live in a world shaped by AI, and so we've used AI tools here. From note-taking and summarizing transcripts to ideating structure, paraphrasing and keeping track of references—AI has been a supportive collaborator.

Authors' Note and Introduction

1. Radjou, Navi, Prabu, Jaideep, and Ahuja, Simone. *Jugaad Innovation: Think Frugal, Be Flexible, Generate Breakthrough Growth*. Jossey-Bass, 2012.

2. Sud, Mukesh, and Narayan, Priyank. *Leapfrog: Six Practices to Thrive*. Penguin Random House India, 2022.

3. 'India's Path to Becoming One of the World's Largest Economies', *Econofact*, 14 July 2025.

4. 'Chapter 1: India's Economic Rise.' *India Economic Strategy to 2035*, Australian Government Department of Foreign Affairs and Trade, 2018.

5. Ries, Eric. *The Lean Startup: How Today's Entrepreneurs Use Continuous Innovation to Create Radically Successful Businesses*. Crown Business, 2011

6. Sarasvathy, Saras D. 'Causation and Effectuation: Toward a Theoretical Shift from Economic Inevitability to Entrepreneurial Contingency', *Academy of Management Review*, vol. 26, no. 2, 2001, pp. 243–263.

7. Rutherford, Ernest. 'We have not got any money, so we have got to think', *Bulletin of the Institute of Physics*, vol. 13, 1962, p. 102 (quoted via R.V. Jones).

Chapter 1.1

1. All quotations from Rahat Kulshreshta, CEO and co-founder of Quidich, are taken from an interview with the authors on 1 June 2024.

2. The name 'Quidich' was born in a dorm room at the Young India Fellowship, where the founders listed every word that captured the spirit of what they were building—fun, high-energy sports, flying drones, competition, cutting-edge tech and some storytelling magic. In that brainstorming session, one word stood out. Inspired by a fictional sport known for its speed, flight and imagination, 'Quidich' perfectly encapsulated everything they believed in.

3. Dew, Nicholas. 'Serendipity in Entrepreneurship', *Organization Studies*, vol. 30, no. 7, 2009, pp. 735–36.

4. Arakali, Harichandan. 'The e-Plane Company: Will India's First Air Taxi Be Electric?', *Forbes India*, 23 November 2021.

5. 'India's ePlane Secures $1bn Air Ambulance Deal', *Airport Technology*, 18 February 2025.

6. Vaitheeswaran, B. 'ePlane Company Gets DGCA Acceptance for Type Certification', *Times of India*, 20 January 2025.

Chapter 1.2

1. All quotations from Chetan Maini, founder of Reva Electric Car Company Ltd, are taken from an interview with the authors on 24 August 2024.

2. 'Meet Mahindra Reva's Chief of Technology Chetan Maini: Pioneer of electric cars in India', *Economic Times*, 29 October 2012.

3. Smith, G. 'On the road: The G-Wiz can tap into that gleeful feeling you had the first time you were allowed

to steer a dodgem on your own', *Guardian,* 29 March 2008.

4. 'The Reva Electric Car Company announces the world premiere of its new Concept Car: REVA-NXG', *The Auto Channel,* 15 April 2005.

5. 'Reva NXG and NXR electric cars', *Car Body Design,* 17 September 2009.

6. AC drive tech refers to an alternating current (AC) motor drive system. This means the car uses an AC motor, typically an induction or synchronous motor, powered by a battery through an inverter that converts the battery's direct current (DC) into AC.

7. Anand Mahindra is the chairman of the Mahindra Group.

8. Evers, A. 'How BYD grew from battery maker to electric vehicle juggernaut, overtaking Tesla', *CNBC,* 26 March 2024.

9. Thakkar, K. 'Renault Kwid receives over 25,000 bookings within 2 weeks since launch, over 40% of buyers are below 28', *Economic Times,* 7 October 2015.

10. Vanham, P. 'Innovation flows from emerging to the developed world', *Financial Times,* 25 May 2017.

Chapter 1.3

1. All quotations from Abhinay Choudhari, co-founder of BigBasket, are taken from an interview with the authors on 30 June 2024.

2. Abraham, S.E. 'I never imagined I would fail, though I never imagined this scale of success either', *Outlook Business*, 30 October 2018.

3. Paul, B. 'Tate acquires majority stake in BigBasket, invests $219 million', *Mint*, 28 May 2021.

4. Abrar, P. 'BigBasket co-founder Abhinay Choudhari launches tech-led laundry service', *Business Standard*, 4 September 2022.

5. Jeon, J. 'Mobile laundry service Laundrygo acquires American company for smart factory upgrades', KoreaTechDesk, 2 June 2021.

6. Biswas, D. 'Winning without VC money: The secret sauce behind Pizza Bakery and Paris Panini's success', YS Life, 27 June 2025.

7. Nair, Sindhu, and S. Smritika. 'The Chai Point ACQT: Brewing Tradition and Technology for Success', *Shanlax International Journal of Management*, 2021.

8. Agrawal, K. 'Drawing parallels between the strategies of Chai Point and Luckin Coffee', Restaurant India.in, 6 February 2020.

9. Anupam, Suprita. 'Chai Point: Blending IoT and AI in Every Cup of Tea', *Inc42*, 21 February 2018.

Chapter 1.4

1. All quotations from Gayatri Srinivas (name changed to maintain confidentiality) are taken from an interview with the authors on 9 September 2024.

2. All quotations from Lalitesh Katragadda are taken from an interview with the authors on 17 August 2024.

3. Kashyaap, S. 'Meet Lalitesh Katragadda, the man behind Google Map Maker, now building tech for India's next billion', *Your Story,* 17 March 2020.

4. Putrevu, S. 'Mapping the journey of Lalitesh Katragadda, the creator of Google Maps India', *Your Story,* 5 February 2018.

5. Katragadda, L. *'Machine Learning for Transliteration',* US Patent US20080221866A1, 11 September 2008.

6. Norman, Don. *The Design of Everyday Things.* Revised and Expanded Edition, Basic Books, 2013.

7. Katragadda, L. 'Making your mark on the world', *Google Official Blog,* 23 June 2008.

8. Blakely, R. 'Google enlists public to map fast changing world', *The Times,* 4 October 2008.

9. Bajwa, A. 'Pakistan tops Google's maps experiment', *The Nation,* 23 May 2009.

10. Aqueel, N. 'Cartography: Tech enthusiasts gear up to map up Karachi', *Tribune,* 11 June 2011.

Chapter 2.1

1. Metwaly, A. 'Sanjoy Roy: You need to be passionate about arts to be able to work in it', *Ahram Online,* 19 April 2014.

2. All quotations from Sanjoy Roy, co-founder of Teamwork Arts, are taken from an interview on 9 January 2025.

3. Bubna, V. 'Namita Gokhale - The name behind Jaipur Literature Festival', *Modern Diplomacy,* 21 April 2022.

4. Chakraborty, S. 'Once a child left for dead, now an award-winning author: Manoranjan Byapari's Remarkable Life', *Reader's Digest*, 21 August 2019.

5. Burke, J. 'Salman Rushdie readings threaten future of Indian literary festival', *Guardian*, 20 January 2012.

6. *Kochi-Muziris Biennale*. Kochi Biennale Foundation, https://www.kochimuzirisbiennale.org/. Accessed 6 October 2025.

7. 'How Guneet Monga Transformed Bollywood', *Bloomberg*, 19 October 2018.

8. Trivedi, Ananya. 'The transnational tales of an Indian creative producer: The case of Guneet Monga.' *Transnational Screens*, vol. 13, no. 3, 2022.

Chapter 2.2

1. All quotations from Sahiba Bali are taken from an interview with the authors on 22 November 2024.

2. 'E170 – The Marketing Masterclass: Ft. Sahiba Bali – From Zomato to Acting', *Indian Silicon Valley with Jivraj Singh Sachar*, aired 14 April 2024.

3. 'Shark Tank India 4: Sharks begin shooting for the new season; Sahiba Bali and Ashish Solanki join as new hosts', *Times Entertainment*, 1 October 2024.

4. All quotations from Surabhi Hodigere are taken from interviews with the authors on 16 November 2024, and 23 November 2024.

5. Mehra, A. 'Society doesn't see women in politics, but I enjoy being the woman in politics' - Surabhi HR, Founder, Political Quotient', *Your Story*, 5 June 2014.

6. Ganapathy, N. 'PM Modi calls on Indian youth to join politics as parties look for fresh faces', *The Straits Times,* 8 September 2024.

7. Easwaran, Eknath, translator. *The Bhagavad Gita: A New Translation.* 2nd ed., Nilgiri Press, 2007.

8. Aurelius, Marcus. *Meditations.* Translated by Gregory Hays, Modern Library, 2006.

Chapter 2.3

1. Abrar, P. 'Traditional VC model not enough for deep science: Social Alpha founder', *Business Standard,* 19 March 2025.

2. All quotations from Manoj Kumar are taken from an interview with the authors on 1 June 2024.

3. 'IIT Kanpur-backed biomaterials startup and D2C wellness brand, Phool.co raises $8M in funding from Sixth Sense Ventures', *IIT Kanpur,* 5 April 2022.

4. Mudur, G.S. 'A decade of building portable MRI scanner', *Telegraph India,* 16 July 2018.

5. 'Voxelgrids Innovations to launch first India-made MRI scanner', *Medical Buyer,* 21 August 2023.

6. All quotations from Rajesh Nair are taken from an interview with the authors on 5 August 2024.

7. Lerner, Josh. *Boulevard of Broken Dreams: Why Public Efforts to Boost Entrepreneurship and Venture Capital Have Failed—and What to Do About It.* Princeton University Press, 2009.

Chapter 2.4

1. All quotations from Shaveta Sharma Kukreja are taken from an interview with the authors on 5 March 2025.

2. Ashish Dhawan is the founder of ChrysCapital, one of India's leading private equity firms, and later the Central Square Foundation (CSF), a pioneering non-profit focused on transforming K–12 education in India. He is also the founding visionary behind Ashoka University, an institution reimagining higher education through interdisciplinary learning and social impact. Dhawan's career exemplifies long-term institution building.

3. Bothra, Neha. 'Forbes India Institution Builder: Ashish Dhawan Is Ensuring Quality Education for Generations', *Forbes India*, 5 March 2025.

4. *Central Square Foundation.* 'About Ashish Dhawan.' https://www.centralsquarefoundation.org/team/ashish-dhawan/. Accessed 6 October 2025

5. Dhawan, Ashish, and Pramath Raj Sinha. 'Reimagining Education Is Key to Future of Work,' *Hindustan Times*, 4 September 2025

6. Pramath Raj Sinha is an educator, entrepreneur, and institution builder with extensive experience across academia, media, and management consulting. He served as the Founding Dean of the Indian School of Business (ISB) He is the Chairman, Board of Trustee of Ashoka University, India's leading liberal arts institution, and has been instrumental in the creation of several higher education initiatives. A former partner at

McKinsey & Company, Sinha's professional trajectory reflects a sustained engagement with institution building in India's evolving education ecosystem.

7. Sinha, Pramath Raj. *Learn, Don't Study: How to Unlock the Power of Learning for Success*. Penguin Random House India, 2019.

8. Ashoka University. 'Founders and Leadership.' https://www.ashoka.edu.in/founders-and-leadership/. Accessed 6 October 2025.

9. BW Online Bureau. 'Pramath Raj Sinha: The Quiet Architect of Indian Higher Education Turns 61', BW Education, 13 June 2025

10. 'How the Founder of ISB, Ashoka University Is Changing India: Pramath Raj Sinha.' YouTube, uploaded by Indian Silicon Valley by Jivraj Singh Sachar, 11 September 2023.

11. Gates, Bill, and Melinda Gates. 'Global Education Grant to Central Square Foundation', *Gates Foundation*, February 2021.

12. Majumdar, D. 'Changing the Game: Using Technology for Foundational Learning', *Central Square Foundation*, 29 September 2019.

13. Anitha, G.F.S., and U. Narasimhan. 'Seeing the National Education Policy 2020 through the Lens of Early Child Development', *Indian Psychiatry Journal*, vol. 30, no. 1, January–June 2021, pp. 182–86.

14. 'Annual Status of Education Report (rural) 2018, 15 January 2019.

15. Harigovind, A. 'Sharp gains in reading and math learning levels in schools across states: ASER 2024', *Indian Express*, 30 January 2025.

16. 'Shaheen Mistri,' Wikipedia, 3 January 2025.

17. 'Case study: Akanksha Foundation Schools', Brookings, 6 May 2023.

18. 'Firki Teach to Lead', Capgemini, https://www.capgemini.com/in-en/wp-content/uploads/sites/18/2025/08/Firki-Teach-To-Lead.pdf. Accessed 6 October 2025

19. Ameshi, A. 'From Classrooms to Changemakers: Inside Teach For India's Movement for Equity in Education', The CSR Universe, 6 June 2025.

20. 'Teaching for India', RSA, 2 December 2022.

Chapter 3.1

1. All quotations from Deepthi Bopaiah are taken from an interview with the authors on 7 September 2024.

2. 'GoSports Foundation announces Deepthi Bopaiah as CEO and Unmish Parthasarathi as Board Member', *Business Standard,* 1 February 2022.

3. Gopalakrishnan, R. 'CSR secrets by GoSports CEO Deepthi Bopaiah', *Sportskeeda,* 2 June 2023.

4. 'Infosys Foundation Collaborates with GoSports Foundation to Launch "Girls for Gold" Program for Aspiring Women Athletes across India', Infosys, 2 May 2023.

5. 'Paris 2024: All medals won by India in Paralympic history', *Sportstar,* 25 August 2024.

6. Peesara, A. 'Paris 2024 Paralympic medal tally: Indian winners from every sport - full list and table', *Olympics,* 8 September 2024.

7. 'Cradle of success: How Odisha brought revolution in India's hockey culture', *New Indian Express,* 30 August 2021.

8. Mao, F. 'Indian teen becomes youngest world chess champion', *BBC News,* 12 December 2024.

9. Chanda, K. 'Mary Kom: Packing a punch, even at 36', *Forbes India,* 1 March 2019.

Chapter 3.2

1. All quotations from Vivek Raghavan are taken from interviews with the authors on 7 January 2024 and 30 August 2024.

2. 'CDLDS seminar series talk - Building Generative AI for (in) India - by Vivek Raghavan (Speaker Bio)', Ashoka University.

3. Beckn is an open protocol developed in India that allows digital platforms like ride-hailing, food delivery and healthcare to interconnect and operate seamlessly, without relying on a single centralized app. It's part of India's effort to build open, interoperable digital infrastructure.

4. 'IIT Madras faculty develop AI to process text in 11 Indian languages', *New Indian Express,* 22 September 2020.

5. 'Sarvam AI: The startup building India's first homegrown Generative AI for every language', *Business Today,* 18 March 2025.

6. 'Sarvam AI launches multilingual, voice enabled GenAI platform supporting 10 Indian languages', *The Hindu Business Line,* 13 August 2024.

7. 'Sarvam AI launches Sarvam-M, India's open weights model for sovereign AI', AI Tech Suite, 23 May 2025.

8. Wodecki, B. 'AI Model for Hindi Speakers Outshines GPT 3.5T in Translations', AI Business, 13 December 2023.

9. Hugging Face is an open-source AI platform and community that hosts thousands of machine learning models, datasets and tools. It's widely used to share and collaborate on natural language processing and generative AI projects.

10. Tokenization is the process of breaking text into smaller pieces—called tokens—so that a language model can understand and process it. Tokens can be as small as individual letters, parts of words or whole words. Since many Indian languages use longer or more complex words, they often get split into more tokens than English, making processing more expensive and slower.

11. 'Meet Krutrim, India's own AI, developed by Ola CEO Bhavish Aggarwal-led venture', *Hindustan Times*, 15 December 2023.

12. Krutrim (meaning 'artificial' in Sanskrit) reflects its focus on sovereign AI, designed specifically for India's unique linguistic, cultural and business needs.

13. Banthia, J. 'Ola's Bhavish Aggarwal unveils 'made for India' Krutrim AI', *The Hindu Business Line*, 15 December 2023.

14. Dalugdud, M. 'Musical AI and Beatoven.ai to jointly launch what they claim to be the first fully licensed AI music generator', *Music Business Worldwide*, 4 December 2024.

15. Stempniak, M. 'Radiology artificial intelligence firm Qure.ai among Time Magazine's "Most Influential Companies in the World" for 2025', *Radiology Business,* 27 June 2025.

16. 'India unveils first fully designed AI server', *The Indian Eye,* 19 April 2025.

Chapter 3.3

1. 'Nilekani to head Unique Database Authority, gets Cabinet rank', *Economic Times,* 25 June 2009.

2. 'Nandan M. Nilekani: Aadhaar Man.' *Startup Talky.* Accessed 6 October 2025.

3. Nilekani, Nandan. *Imagining India: Ideas for the New Century.* Penguin Books, 2012.

4. All quotations from Nandan Nilekani are taken from interviews with Prof. Jaideep Prabhu on 18 July 2017 and 14 July 2023.

5. Perrigo, B. 'India has been collecting eye scans and fingerprint records from every citizen. Here's what to know.', *Time,* 28 September 2018.

6. Gelb, A., and Diofasi, A. 'Ghostbusters: Linking Subsidy Reform and Biometric Identification in India', Center for Global Development, 17 March 2015.

7. Goel, Anusha. 'An Empirical Study of Jan Dhan - Aadhaar - Mobile Trinity and Financial Inclusion', *International Journal of Banking Risk and Insurance,* 2020, 8, pp. 62–79.

8. Sudhir, K., and Sunder, S. 'What happens when a billion identities are digitized', *Yale Insights,* 27 March 2020.

9. 'Aadhaar Enrollment Cost Lowest in India: Report', *Business Standard*, 9 June 2015.

10. Federal Authority for Identity, Citizenship, Customs & Port Security. Emirates ID Information Portal. Government of the United Arab Emirates.

11. Government Accountability Office (GAO). REAL ID Implementation: Status and Cost Estimates. GAO Report, 2019, pp. 19–391.

12. Government of Kenya. Huduma Namba Registration. Government of Kenya.

13. US Department of Homeland Security. REAL ID Act Implementation. US DHS.

14. US Department of Homeland Security. REAL ID: State-by-State Cost Overview.

15. '2 Biggest Reasons, as per Infosys Co-founder Nandan Nilekani, That Helped UPI Become One of the World's Biggest Payment Modes', *Times of India*, 19 February 2023.

16. 'UPI, AA, and ONDC Will Reorder Indian Supply Chains: Nandan Nilekani', *Economic Times*, 20 September 2022.

17. PAHAL (Pratyaksh Hanstantrit Labh) Scheme, also known as the Direct Benefit Transfer for LPG (DBTL) scheme, which aims to transfer the LPG subsidy directly into the bank accounts of beneficiaries.

18. Romer, Paul. 'India's Aadhaar Is the Most Sophisticated ID Programme in the World', *Times of India*, 22 April 2017.

19. 'Unified Payments Interface (UPI)', National Payments Corporation of India.

20. 'UIDAI slashes Aadhaar authentication charge to ₹3: CEO', *The Hindu*, 29 September 2021.

21. Chadha, S. 'India home to 26 fintech uniforms with a combined market value of $90 bn', *Business Standard*, 3 September 2024.

22. Toshniwal, A. 'Monthly transactions on ONDC to hit around 50 million by the end of the year: CEO Koshy', *Your Story*, 29 May 2024.

23. Choudhury, D. 'Ola, Uber challenger Namma Yatri crosses 5mn users, $50mn in driver earnings', *Money Control*, 28 February 2024.

24. 'India's Beckn Protocol: An Open Network Digital Stack Is the Flavour of the World.' *Mysuru Infra Hub*, 2024.

25. Reserve Bank Innovation Hub (RBIH). Unified Lending Interface (ULI), 2024.

26. Raghavan, Vivek. *India Stack Presentation.* ThoughtWorks, 2019.

27. 'Unified Lending Interface Is in Pilot Stage, Will Be Launched Nationwide in Due Course, Says RBI Governor Shaktikanta Das', *Economic Times*, 26 August 2024.

28. Unified Energy Interface Alliance (UEI Alliance). About the Unified Energy Interface, 2024.

Chapter 3.4

1. 'Time to Unlearn Jugaad and Embrace Sustainable Innovation', *The Hindu*, 15 September 2023.

2. 'Mangalyaan: India's race for space success', *BBC News*, 24 September 2014.

3. 'India's first Mars satellite "Mangalyaan" enters orbit', *BBC News,* 24 September 2014.

4. 'Chandrayaan-3 Project Cost at ₹600 Cr Lower than Budgets of Some Hollywood Films on Space, Says Union Minister', *Economic Times,* 2023.

5. 'ISRO's Office Was Once a Church, and Its Launchpad a Beach', *Condé Nast Traveller India,* n.d.

6. 'How ISRO Has Developed Its Low-Cost Edge', *Economic Times,* 24 August 2023.

7. 'Frugal Engineering: Why ISRO's Mars Mission Is the Cheapest', *Economic Times,* 5 November 2013.

8. 'India's Mars Orbiter Mission: The Frugal Innovation', *Financial Express,* 25 September 2014.

9. 'India's Mission to Mars Cost Less than the Movie Gravity', *Vox,* 24 September 2014.

10. 'India's Mars Mission Cost Less than Hollywood Film Gravity: PM Narendra Modi', *Times of India,* 30 June 2014.

11. 'What Makes India's Space Missions Cost Less than Hollywood Sci-Fi Movies?' *Business Standard,* 2023.

12. 'How India Achieves Cost-Efficient Space Missions to the Moon and Mars', *Jade Times,* 2023.

13. 'How ISRO Challenges Global Space Mission Budgets: 7 Projects That Shocked the World with Their Cost-Effectiveness', *Moneycontrol,* 2023.

14. 'Efficiency in Space: ISRO's Budgetary Triumph', *Indigenesis,* 2023.

15. Petrova, M. 'How China's satellite megaprojects are challenging Elon Musk's Starlink', CNBC, 15 December 2024.

16. John, N. 'Raise the Space Bar: As SpaceX provides some of cheapest satellite launches, what can ISRO do to reclaim cost advantage?', *Economic Times*, 3 November 2024.

17. Space Exploration Technologies Corp. (SpaceX). Falcon 9., n.d.

18. 'HAL-L&T Consortium to Build Five PSLV Rockets for ISRO', *The Hindu*, 5 September 2022.

19. 'Anuradha T.K.' Wikipedia, n.d. Accessed 24 December 2024.

20. 'India's Space Strategy: Harness Data and Tiny Satellites to Capture Market beyond SpaceX', *Reuters*, 14 October 2024.

21. 'Minal Rohit,' Wikipedia, n.d. Accessed 24 December 2024.

22. 'All the Women Scientists and Engineers in ISRO Team Who Worked on Chandrayaan Three like Ritu Karidhal', *iDiva*, n.d. Accessed 24 December 2024.

23. Indian Space Research Organization (ISRO). Mars Orbiter Mission (Mangalyaan)., n.d.

24. Singh, R. 'ISRO's Mars Orbiter Mission: A Triumph of Frugality', *Hindustan Times*, 23 September 2014.

Conclusion & Frugal Innovation Canvas

1. Global Ecobrick Alliance. 'What Is an Ecobrick?' *Ecobricks*. Accessed 4 October 2025.

2. Maier, Russell. 'This Canadian Accidentally Discovered How to Solve Our Plastic Problem', Interview by Christa I. De La Cruz, *SPOT.ph*, 10 August 2017.

3. Hopkins, Rob. 'EcoBricks and Education: How Plastic Bottle Rubbish Is Helping Build Schools', *Guardian*, 29 May 2014.

4. Global Ecobrick Alliance. 'Why Make Ecobricks?' *Ecobricks*. Accessed 16 November 2024.

5. 'Into Ecobricks', *Plan 4 Plastic*, 9 September 2014. Accessed 18 March 2025.

6. Global Ecobrick Alliance. '10 Step Guide to Making an Ecobrick', *Ecobricks*. Accessed 16 November 2024.

7. Maier, Russell, and Ani Himawati. *The Rise of the Regenerative Ecobrick Movement*, 2021.

8. Wardani, Farida, and Nurul Khotimah. 'Making Eco-Bricks as a Solution to Environmental Problems through Empowering Creative Children: A Case Study in Baruga District, Kendari City', *International Journal of Science and Society*, vol. 3, no. 2, 2021, pp. 214–21. doi:10.54783/ijsoc.v3i2.331.

9. ISRO faced international sanctions after India's nuclear tests, which raised global concerns about the dual use of space and nuclear technologies.

10. Smith, Wendy K., and Marianne W. Lewis. *Both/And Thinking: Embracing Creative Tensions to Solve Your Toughest Problems*. Harvard Business Review Press, 2022.

11. Smith, Wendy K., and Marianne W. Lewis. 'Toward a Theory of Paradox: A Dynamic Equilibrium Model of Organizing', *Academy of Management Review*, vol. 36, no. 2, 2011, pp. 381–403.

12. Martin, Roger L. *The Opposable Mind: How Successful Leaders Win Through Integrative Thinking*. Harvard Business School Press, 2007.

13. Stokes, Patricia D. *Creativity from Constraints: The Psychology of Breakthrough*. Springer, 2005.

14. Brooks, Cleanth. 'The Language of Paradox.' *The Well Wrought Urn: Studies in the Structure of Poetry*. Harcourt, Brace, 1947, pp. 3–21.

15. Cowling, Elizabeth. *Picasso: Style and Meaning*. Phaidon, 2002.

16. Radjou, Navi, and Jaideep Prabhu. *Frugal Innovation: How to Do Better with Less*. Profile Books, 2015.

17. Orzel, Chad. 'Does a New Paradox Offer Hope for Progress in Quantum Foundations?', *Forbes*, 21 September 2018.

18. Rothenberg, Albert. 'The Janusian Process in Scientific Creativity', *Creativity Research Journal*, vol. 9, nos. 2–3, 1996, pp. 207–31.

19. 'Effectuation', Effectuation.org.

20. Sato, Yasuhito. 'Mottainai: A Japanese Sense of *Anima Mundi*', *History of Psychiatry*, 2017.

21. Ohno, Taiichi. *Toyota Production System: Beyond Large-Scale Production*. Productivity Press, 1988.

22. Rangan, V. Kasturi. 'Aravind Eye Hospital, Madurai, India: In Service for Sight', Harvard Business School Case 593-098, April 1993.

23. McKinsey & Company. 'Driving Down the Cost of High-Quality Care: Aravind Eye Care System', *Health International*, no. 11, 2011.

24. Molina, Anton, Anesta Kothari, Alex Odundo, and Manu Prakash. 'Agave sisalana: Towards Distributed Manufacturing of Absorbent Media for Menstrual Pads

in Semi-Arid Regions', *Communications Engineering*, vol. 2, no. 1, 2023.

25. Ries, Eric. *The Lean Startup: How Today's Entrepreneurs Use Continuous Innovation to Create Radically Successful Businesses.* Crown Business, 2011.

26. The Frugal Innovation Canvas that we propose draws its structural inspiration from Alexander Osterwalder and Yves Pigneur's Business Model Canvas (2010). Much like the original, it serves as a one-page visual framework that helps innovators systematically think through the essential components of their ideas.

27. Osterwalder, Alexander, and Yves Pigneur. *Business Model Generation: A Handbook for Visionaries, Game Changers, and Challengers.* John Wiley & Sons, 2010.

28. Prahalad, C.K.. and R.A. Mashelkar. 'Innovation's Holy Grail', *Harvard Business Review*, 88(7/8), 2010, pp. 132–141.

29. Borde, Sushil and R.A. Mashelkar. *More from Less for More.* Penguin Random House India, 2025.

Visit www.leansparkbook.com for more stories and a downloadable PDF of the Frugal Innovation Canvas (FIC).

The authors can be reached at:

j.prabhu@jbs.cam.ac.uk
priyank.narayan@ashoka.edu.in
mukeshs@iima.ac.in

Scan QR code to access the
Penguin Random House India website